experience and a passion for trav

**Rely on Thomas Cook as your
travelling companion on your next trip
and benefit from our unique heritage.**

Thomas Cook **pocket** guides

SEVILLE

Written by Nick Inman
Updated by Michelle Chaplow

Published by Thomas Cook Publishing
A division of Thomas Cook Tour Operations Limited
Company registration No: 3772199 England
The Thomas Cook Business Park, 9 Coningsby Road
Peterborough PE3 8SB, United Kingdom
Email: books@thomascook.com, Tel: +44 (0)1733 416477
www.thomascookpublishing.com

Produced by The Content Works Ltd
Aston Court, Kingsmead Business Park, Frederick Place
High Wycombe, Bucks HP11 1LA
www.thecontentworks.com

Series design based on an original concept by Studio 183 Limited

ISBN: 978-1-84848-302-6

First edition © 2006 Thomas Cook Publishing
This third edition © 2010 Thomas Cook Publishing
Text © Thomas Cook Publishing
Maps © Thomas Cook Publishing/PCGraphics (UK) Limited
Transport map © Communicarta Limited

Series Editor: Kelly Pipes
Production/DTP: Steven Collins

Printed and bound in Spain by GraphyCems

Cover photography (Flamenco dancers) © Theo Fitzhugh/Alamy

CONTENTS

SYMBOLS KEY

The following symbols are used throughout this book:

ⓐ address ☎ telephone ⓦ website address 🕒 opening times
🅝 public transport connections ❗ important

The following symbols are used on the maps:

𝒊	information office	▓	points of interest
✈	airport	○	city
✚	hospital	○	large town
🕒	police station	○	small town
🚌	bus station	═	motorway
🚆	railway station	━	main road
Ⓜ	metro	─	minor road
Ⓣ	tram	—	railway
✝	cathedral		
❶	numbers denote featured cafés & restaurants		

Hotels and restaurants are graded by approximate price as follows:
£ budget price ££ mid-range price £££ expensive

Abbreviations used in addresses:

Av.	Avenida (Avenue)
C/	Calle (Street)
Pl.	Plaza (Square)

▶ *The arches of the Real Alcázar*

INTRODUCING
Seville

Introduction

If any city can encapsulate the colour, sensuality, vitality and carefree spirit of southern Europe, it has to be Seville. It's a place that leaves few visitors cold. Rather, most of them feel compelled towards glowing superlatives. Camilo José Cela, Spain's Nobel Prize-winning novelist, declared it a city capable of inspiring even the dullest of poets. The travel writer Nina Epton, meanwhile, observed that 'the most abstemious of visitors feels inebriated in Seville'.

Spain's fourth-largest city and the capital of the region of Andalucia, it's the only city in the country to sit astride a major river, the great, green-flowing Guadalquivir River, 60 navigable kilometres (37 miles) inland from the Atlantic coast.

Seville's long and eventful history – particularly the days when gold flowed incessantly from Spain's New World colonies – has left it filled with innumerable monuments. Most conspicuous of them is the Giralda Tower, which rises out of the cathedral as a Muslim minaret and finishes as a Christian belfry.

Down at ground level, the biggest draws are the exquisite palace of the Real Alcázar; the quaint Barrio de Santa Cruz, a perfect cluster of narrow, shady streets through which the fragrance of orange blossom wafts delicately in spring; the legendary Maestranza Bullring; and, more viscerally, the music, dynamism and song of flamenco whose exciting, passionate presence is felt all over the city. Such are the ingredients that gave birth to the fictional characters of Carmen and Don Juan, Seville's most famous inhabitants.

It would be a mistake to see Seville as merely a city living on myths of *toreros*, libertines and gypsy flamenco dancers. Seville is – and likes to think of itself as – a thoroughly modern, hard-working city. Twice in the last hundred years (in 1929 and 1992) it has held international exhibitions to convince the world that it is up with the contemporary zeitgeist. While both have left the city with some interesting pieces of architecture, neither has made much impact on traditional Seville. This is a city that will probably leave you guessing what is real and what is cliché.

🔺 *The golden horizons of the Torre del Oro*

When to go

There is no wrong time to visit Seville, but bear in mind that July and August can be challenging as the (sometimes oppressive) heat drives many residents to decamp to the coast and, as a consequence, quite a few bars and cafés can close without warning. Spring is a particularly lovely time to visit because of the blossom and flowers in parks and gardens.

SEASONS & CLIMATE

This is southern Spain and you can expect it to be anything from agreeably warm to unpleasantly hot. Even in the thick of winter it rarely gets truly cold, and overcast or rainy days are the exception rather than the rule.

ANNUAL EVENTS

Southern Spain has a busy calendar of traditional fiestas. In Seville the two most important are Holy Week (see below) and, immediately after it, the April Fair (see page 12).

March & April

Semana Santa (Holy Week) Holy Week is celebrated all over Spain, but nowhere to the extent that you'll witness in Seville, where processions and street parties make for high-octane merriment. Events take place throughout the week, but the best times to take part are Maundy Thursday night and very early on Good Friday morning.

La Feria de Abril (The April Fair) A flamboyant *feria* of flamenco fun that fills the city with colour and joy (see The April Fair, page 12).

🔺 *Semana Santa procession in Seville*

May & June
El Rocío On Whitsunday (some time between mid-May and mid-June, depending on the date of Easter) the little town of El Rocío (see page 108) is swamped by an army of thousands of traditionally costumed pilgrims to honour the Virgen del Rocío (Virgin of the Dew).

September & October
Feria de San Miguel A fair in which the city revisits some of its cultural traditions with displays of horsemanship and bullfighting

● *Parading the Virgin during the city's patron saint festival*

prowess at the Fundación Real Escuela Andaluza de Arte Ecuestre (Royal Horse School, see page 110).

Flamenco Biennial (mid-Sept–mid-Oct on even-numbered years) Displays, shows and even academic conferences celebrate the joyous gypsy dance at venues throughout the city. The festival has been running since 1980 and gets bigger and better each time. Book accommodation well in advance.

December

Fiesta de La Virgen de La Inmaculada (7 & 8 Dec) Choirs and teams of dancers – including, on the second day, children – pay tribute to the city's patron saint. ➋ Pl. de Triunfo

PUBLIC HOLIDAYS
Año Nuevo (New Year's Day) 1 Jan
Día de Reyes (Epiphany) 6 Jan
Día de Andalucía 28 Feb
Jueves Santo & Viernes Santo (Maundy Thursday & Good Friday) 21 & 22 Apr 2011, 5 & 6 Apr 2012, 28 & 29 Mar 2013
Día del Trabajo (Labour Day) 1 May
Virgen de los Reyes (patroness of the city; the Day of the Assumption) 15 Aug
Día de la Hispanidad (Spain's national day) 12 Oct
Todos Los Santos (All Saints' Day) 1 Nov
Día de la Constitución (Constitution Day) 6 Dec
La Inmaculada Concepción (Immaculate Conception) 8 Dec
Día de Navidad (Christmas Day) 25 Dec

The April Fair

Immediately after the excesses of Holy Week, Seville launches into an altogether different type of celebration. There's nothing religious about the April Fair. It's simply an enormous party, six intense days of hyperactivity mainly celebrating Andalucian folk culture. It's held in the fairground in the Barrio de los Remedios. Just follow the tide of people (including women in gaudy flamenco dresses) across the Puente San Telmo from Parque María Luisa or through Triana and you'll find the monumental gateway of lights.

You're welcome to wander around the streets of the fairground and savour the atmosphere, but you'll soon realise that the fair is a combination of private parties taking place in *casetas* (marquees) that are members-only, owned by societies, companies, families and other organisations. What's more, they are often patrolled by security personnel. Fortunately a few *casetas* – notably those owned by political parties – are open to the public and are essentially makeshift bars, which can easily get crowded. Most of the larger *casetas* are equipped with a dance floor. The soundtrack of the fair is the *sevillana*, a home-grown variant of flamenco.

Between 12.00 and 20.00 there is a steady stream of horse riders and horse-drawn carriages rumbling around the fairground in what is known as the *Paseo de Caballos*, or Horse Procession. Cocky *señoritos* (wearing the typical Andalucian herdsman's outfit of grey, wide-brimmed hat, tight leather breeches and a short jacket) will already be knocking back glasses of *fino* sherry, the fair's preferred tipple.

The music and the dancing get going only in the evening after the bullfight in the Plaza de Toros de la Real Maestranza (see page 81), considered an integral part of the fair. It is not just that the fairground is transformed into a spectacle of illuminations by the lanterns, or *farolillos*, along its streets, it's also that at night you are more likely to catch a glimpse of aristocrats, bullfighters, pop stars and other Spanish celebrities drawn by the glamour of the fair.

Seville's fair is undoubtedly the fair to attend, but if you can't make it or you want something less exclusive, try the fair at Jerez de la Frontera (see page 110), which is held shortly afterwards and whose *casetas* are mostly open to the public.

⬥ *On horseback at the April Fair*

History

Local tradition insists that Hercules, the Greek mythological hero, founded Seville. In reality, though, it was Julius Caesar who, in 45 BC, raised what was probably a small Iberian settlement on the banks of the Guadalquivir to the status of Roman municipality. By the fourth century AD, Hispalis (as it was then known) was one of the most important cities in Spain. But as the Roman Empire crumbled, it was captured by invading hordes of barbarians: first the Vandals, then the Visigoths. Two local clergymen, saints Leander and Isidore, were instrumental in winning the latter away from the Arian heresy and over to mainstream Christianity.

When Muslim (usually known as Moorish) invaders overran Spain from North Africa in 711 they were quick to take the city, which they renamed Isbilya. In the 11th century it became capital of a kingdom that stretched from modern-day Portugal to the east coast of Spain. A fresh wave of Muslim invaders, the Almohads, made Seville their capital, and the city enjoyed another brief moment of splendour of which the famous Giralda Tower is the chief reminder.

In 1248 King Fernando III of Castile took Seville for Christianity and made it his residence. The city's mosques were converted into churches. One of his successors, Pedro I, was responsible for building the magnificent royal palace of the Real Alcázar.

With the fall of Granada in 1492 the Reconquest of Spain was complete. That same year Columbus was dispatched on his historic voyage to the Americas. As a river port close to the Atlantic seaboard, Seville was ideally placed to profit from growing trade with the New World, and the city grew rich on the proceeds.

The good times ended in 1717 when Seville lost its monopoly to nearby Cádiz. The next centuries were hard for the economically struggling city beset by plague and floods. Its woes increased with the loss of Spain's colonies and valuable trade.

In 1929 Seville tried to rebrand itself by staging a Latin American Expo which left little behind except the Parque María Luisa and some elegant architecture. Then came the devastating Spanish Civil War of 1936–9, which was finally won after much bloodshed by the Nationalists, led by military *generalísimo* Francisco Franco. Franco ruled Spain as an oppressive dictator for 36 years until his death in 1975. The country only recovered with the advent of democracy and a new constitution; shortly afterwards, widespread devolution meant that Seville became the capital of Andalucia. Soon after that, a local boy, Felipe Gonzalez, became prime minister of Spain.

With prime minister José Luis Rodríguez Zapatero heading Spain's socialist government and the royal family as popular as ever, things are going generally well for the country as a whole – despite the inevitable economic problems caused by the global financial crisis of 2008-2009 and an ongoing struggle with immigration.

Andalucia is going from strength to strength and this development can be seen in Seville's rapidly improving infrastructure: in the last decade, buildings of architectural, cultural and historical significance have been carefully renovated, many streets in the historic centre are now totally pedestrianised and there have been massive improvements in the field of transport. Bicycle lanes, a metro system and a state-of-the-art tram line have succeeded in reducing traffic in the city and creating superb open public spaces adorned with elegant street furniture. It comes as no surprise that this well-maintained, elegant city is still often referred to as the Jewel of Andalucia.

Lifestyle

Sevillanos like to think they are hard-working, but they are also proud of their capacity for going at their own pace and enjoying themselves. The climate imposes a certain rhythm to life and you'll be wise to go with it – particularly in summer when the heat makes it difficult to do anything in a hurry.

A Seville day begins slowly and the morning is long. Lunchtime is late compared with most other countries. Only touristy restaurants start serving before 14.00 and it is not unusual to sit down to a full meal after 15.00.

A long digestive break follows with or without a siesta according to personal preference and the weather. In the summer it makes sense to take a nap in the heat of the day so as to be refreshed and ready to go out when the temperature becomes bearable again in the evening.

The afternoon begins at 16.00–17.00 and many people still have half a working day ahead of them before clocking off at around 21.00.

Dinner is around 22.00–23.00, but is not as heavy as lunch. If the gap between meals becomes interminable, you can always fill it with a few tapas.

To keep up with the locals it's best to adjust to their rhythm and do as they do. Don't try to do everything in one day, give yourself occasional time off, and be prepared for a late night if you want to see the city at its most relaxed.

Although some of the locals can seem brusque at times this is often because they are slightly fazed by dealing with so many tourists who don't speak their language. Most people you meet will be only too helpful. Keep a smile on your face, adopt the local manners and don't be too quick to take offence and you'll get what you want. Particularly important in this gregarious country is to show respect for other people. Always say 'hello' when you enter a shop, bar or any other public place: *buenos días* during the day and *buenas tardes* (good afternoon/evening) from 19.00–20.00 onwards. And don't forget to say *adiós* when you leave.

◔ *Enjoy a leisurely lunch on the terrace of El Faro de Triana (see page 100)*

Culture

Although Seville is a modern city with a contemporary culture, it takes most of its inspiration from the past and from its tradition. In particular, its greatest creative age was the 17th century, the period of baroque when New World riches paid for artworks to furnish palaces, churches and monasteries. One of Spain's greatest painters, Velázquez, was born in Seville although he spent the greater part of his life around the court in Madrid. Much more intimately associated with the city of their birth are the painters Francisco de Zurbarán (1598–1662), Bartolomé Murillo (1617–82) and Juan de Valdés Leal (1662–95), and the sculptor Juan Martínez Montañez (1568–1648). Invariably, given the times in which they lived, these artists were commissioned to portray religious themes but there is great variety in their approaches. While Murillo, for instance, often verges on sentimentality, Zurbarán is widely thought to have brought a sense of spirituality to his work and Valdés Leal's paintings are strikingly expressive and dramatic, executed with a decisive hand and exploiting strong contrasts in colour and shade.

Seville has two other cultural streams of influence that were once looked down on but have recently acquired respectability. One of these is the music and dance of flamenco, which originated as a marginal gypsy form of song and dance but which has now been assimilated into the mainstream and exported all over the world.

The other cultural revival concerns Seville's Muslim (and to some extent Jewish) past. The Christian Reconquest of Spain at the end of the 15th century was meant to be the definitive end of the Moors and their civilisation, and thereafter few people were interested in

Don Juan, Seville's most famous (or infamous) literary son

anything not born out of Catholic Christianity. But since the death of Franco (a devout Catholic) and the restoration of democracy, Seville has been busy unearthing and putting on display various treasures from its former Muslim self. From time to time there are exhibitions on Al Andalus (Muslim Spain) in venues in Seville, but there are also some permanent reminders that the Christians weren't the only ones to leave us with evidence of an acute artistic sensibility. Several churches have strongly suggestive traces – not to mention emphatic statements – in their architecture and ornamentation of the mosques that they once were.

DON JUAN

The fictional character of archetypal, heart-stealing lecher, Don Juan, 'the Trickster of Seville', was dreamt up by priest and playwright Tirso de Molina in the early 17th century. His creation soon acquired a life of its own. Indeed, he stars in subsequent works by Molière, Mozart and George Bernard Shaw among others, and appears in books, films and even a ballet. More than just an unchecked Latin lover, Don Juan is a complex person who has been described as very un-Spanish in the way he destructively pursues his own goals without regard to the norms of society. 'He is hardly a character at all – but a universal day-dream or myth,' wrote VS Pritchett, who went on to reveal perhaps more about himself than Don Juan by adding: 'He expresses the male desire for inexhaustible sexual vitality, the female desire to be ravished against the will, reason, interest or honour.'

The inner courtyard of the Palacio de Lebrija

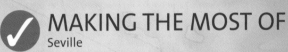

MAKING THE MOST OF
Seville

Shopping

The city's main shopping area centres on two more or less parallel streets, Sierpes and Tetuán (called Velázquez at the northern end). These run from Plaza San Francisco and Plaza Nueva north to the squares of La Campana and Duque de la Victoria. The shops also spread down neighbouring streets towards Plaza Alfalfa and, in the opposite direction, towards the river. Here you'll find just about everything you'll need: men's and women's fashions, shoes, ceramics and other crafts, jewellery and assorted souvenirs. Seville city centre still has many fascinating smaller, and specialised, shops that haven't yet been driven out by national and international brand-name chain stores.

If you don't know where else to look, try El Corte Inglés department store on Plaza del Duque de la Victoria (see page 69) or one of the big three shopping centres: Plaza de Armas (closest to the centre, see page 87), Nervión Plaza (see page 87) or **Los Arcos** (ⓦ www.cclosarcos.com) (further out, continuing past Nervión Plaza).

By far the best street market is El Jueves, which is held, as its name says, on Thursdays from 09.00–14.00 in Calle Feria, La Macarena.

🔺 *A hand-painted fan is a wonderful souvenir*

Principally, it's an antiques market but there are many smaller collectable items for sale and, if nothing else, it's worth attending for the atmosphere.

Craft goods associated with Seville include ceramics (see page 97), *mantones* (shawls, for going out at night or attending the April Fair, see page 12), lace *mantillas* (traditionally worn during Holy Week and by bridesmaids), *bordados* (embroidery), *encajes* (lacework), fans (often hand-painted), guitars, and flamenco dresses and accessories. Other possible items to take home are bullfighting posters, religious statues, olive oil, wine, sherry and cured Spanish hams.

USEFUL SHOPPING PHRASES

What time do the shops open/close?
¿A qué hora abren/cierran las tiendas?
¿A kay ora abren/theeyerran las teeyendas?

How much is this?
¿Cuánto vale?
¿Cwantoe baleh?

Can I try this on?
¿Puedo probarme esto?
¿Pwedo probarme esto?

My size is ...
Mi número es el ...
Mee noomairo es el ...

I'll take this one, thank you
Me llevo éste, gracias
Meh llievo esteh, gratheeas

This is too large/too small/too expensive. Do you have any others?
Es muy grande/muy pequeño/muy caro. ¿Tienen otros?
Es mooy grandeh/mooy pekenio/mooy karo. ¿Teeyenen ohtross?

Eating & drinking

Installing yourself in a succession of bars, cafés and restaurants is one of the delights of a visit to Seville. The city has a wide choice of places to eat and drink – from the old-fashioned and quaint, to the vibrantly modern.

The city takes pride in its number and variety of bars and restaurants catering for all tastes and budgets. They go by several different names – including *asador* (indicating that meat is roasted

⬤ *Locals enjoy a drink in El Rinconcillo (see page 89)*

PRICE CATEGORIES

The price guides given whenever a restaurant is mentioned indicate the approximate price of a three-course meal (*menú del día* if there is one) for one person, excluding drinks, but including tax.

£ up to €20   ££ €20–40   £££ over €40

in a wood-fired oven), *mesón* (an antiquated word for an inn), *cervezería* (specialising in beers) and *bodega* or *bodeguita* (specialising in wines).

For the most part, the cuisine is 'typically Andalucian' – which means straightforward meat, fish, seafood and vegetable dishes prepared and served with the minimum of complication and formality. With such an abundance of good fresh ingredients to hand there's no need to disguise them with rich sauces. As this is southern Spain most dishes have olive oil lurking in them somewhere and dairy foods are used minimally.

If you don't like the local food or want a change from it, the city has a good choice of restaurants specialising in the cuisines of other parts of Spain and an array of international restaurants including Chinese, Japanese, Latin American, Italian and, inevitably, fast food.

The main meal in Spain is eaten in the middle of the day. This is when most restaurants offer a cheaper menu, *menú del día*, which typically consists of three courses with a glass of the house wine included. This is certainly the best way to fill up without spending a lot of money. Note that a *menú de degustación* is something altogether different. Only seen in high-class restaurants, it is a pricey sampler menu.

Where Seville excels is in its tapas bars, the fast-food joints of Spain. Even posh restaurants are likely to have a bar attached where you can eat well without having to order a full meal. Order what you want – if you want a larger portion ask for a *ración* of it – and pay for what you have eaten and drunk at the end. But take care: tapas can easily add up to more than the cost of a *menú del día*. The big thing about tapas is that they are available any time of day or night. You'll never hear anyone in Seville tell you the kitchen is closed and there's nothing to eat!

Tapas are often a godsend to vegetarians visiting Spain. If nothing else, almost every bar can provide a *ración* of meat-free salad or a slice of the old stand-by, *tortilla de patata* (potato omelette).

To go with the tapas, Spain has an increasingly good choice of wines, many of them economically priced. Imported bottles, by contrast, are rarely seen and are expensive. If there is a Sevillian drink par excellence, it has to be *fino* sherry – a dry fortified wine made in Jerez and drunk chilled.

Spain's main gastronomic failing is its dessert menu, which all too often reduces to a piece of fresh fruit, a scoop of ice cream or the ubiquitous *flan* – crème caramel. But it makes up for this deficiency by being strong on sweet snacks. Seville has several excellent cake shops, *pastelerías*, offering a choice of something to go with a coffee or to fill the long gap between lunch and dinner. The best known of them is La Campana (see page 72).

Another weak point for many visitors – particularly British – is breakfast. Many Spaniards eat hardly anything when they first get up, preferring instead to have a sandwich or snack mid-morning. A few bars do open early and serve a reasonably good breakfast of toast, coffee and fresh orange juice. A popular alternative to this is a portion of *churros* – deep fried sticks of batter that are sprinkled with sugar and dunked into a cup of coffee or hot chocolate.

USEFUL DINING PHRASES

I would like a table for ... people
Quisiera una mesa para ... personas
Keyseeyera oona mesa para ... personas

May I have the bill, please?
¿Podría traerme la cuenta
por favor?
*¿Podreea tryairme la cwenta
por fabor?*

Waiter/waitress!
¡Camarero/Camarera!
¡Camareroe/Camarera!

Could I have it well-cooked/medium/rare please?
¿Por favor, la carne bien hecha/al punto/poco hecha?
¿Por fabor, la kahrneh beeyen etcha/al poontoh/poko etcha?

I am a vegetarian. Does this contain meat?
Soy vegetariano/a (fem.) ¿Tiene carne este plato?
Soy behetahreeahnoh/ah. ¿Teeyeneh carneh esteh plahtoh?

Where is the toilet (restroom) please?
¿Dónde están los servicios, por favor?
¿Dondeh estan los serbeetheeos, por fabor?

I would like a cup of/two cups of/another coffee/tea
Quisiera una taza de/dos tazas de/otra taza de café/té
*Keyseeyera oona tatha dey/dos tathas dey/otra tatha
dey kafey/tey*

Entertainment & nightlife

Largely due to the climate, but also because of the pattern of
the working day, nights out begin late in Seville and go on later –
especially in summer when daytime temperatures are too hot
to do anything except cower indoors.

● *Ceramic mural depicting a typical flamenco scene*

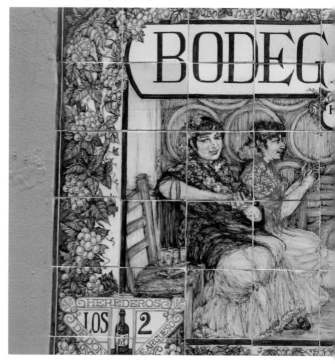

At any time of year the street life may be enough to entertain you, but there are always regular live-performance venues to draw you in complemented by a busy programme of special events. Everything is listed or advertised in various publications available free from tourist information offices. The best and most complete of them is *El Giraldillo*, which is almost entirely in Spanish but still intelligible to a non-speaker.

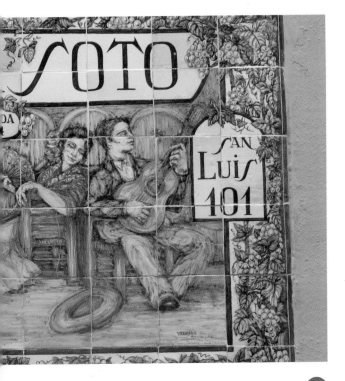

The largest entertainment venue in the city is the **Auditorio Municipal Rocío Jurado** (ⓐ Camino de los Descubrimientos, Isla de la Cartuja ⓣ (954) 46 71 70), named after the late Rocío Jurado, a legendary Spanish singer nicknamed 'La Más Grande' (The Greatest). Tickets and listings information can be obtained from El Corte Inglés (see page 69).

The city's three main theatres (all of which sometimes have concerts to complement their programmes of plays) are, in order of artistic significance:

Teatro Central (ⓐ C/ José de Gálvez 6, Isla de la Cartuja ⓣ (955) 03 72 00 ⓦ www.teatrocentral.com), **Teatro Lope de Vega** (ⓐ Av. María Luisa ⓣ (955) 47 28 22 ⓦ www.teatrolopedevega.org) and **Teatro de la Maestranza** (ⓐ Paseo Colón 22 ⓣ (954) 22 65 73 ⓦ www.teatromaestranza.com).

La Imperdible theatre company (ⓣ (954) 38 82 19 ⓦ www.imperdible.org) is a small, innovative, independent group which performs in **Teatro Duque** (ⓐ Pl. del Duque de la Victoria ⓣ (954) 90 54 58) until their planned new theatre opens on Calle Torneo.

The two golden rules for enjoying the nightlife of Seville are not to go out too early – certainly not before 23.00 – and not to drink too much. Many people like to start the evening in one or more *bares de copas*. These are bars for drinking (shorts rather than beers and wines) which don't generally serve tapas. They can be distinguished from everyday bars not only by their late opening hours but also because they have few chairs, not too much light, preened bar staff and loud music on the speakers, possibly controlled by a DJ. Only after midnight or later do people move on to the clubs – although be sure to call them *discotecas* because 'club' in Spanish sometimes has connotations of a roadside brothel.

FLAMENCO

Flamenco is the music, song and dance of Andalucia, particularly of the gypsy community. It is associated especially with the provinces of Seville and Cádiz. The rough wailing voice of the singer is often unaccompanied except by rhythmic clapping, but to this is often added the rapid strumming of a guitar. Songs are never less than full-on passionate and express a range of emotions, mainly sadness and torment. Sometimes the singer and guitarist provide the soundtrack for a dancer – usually female. In true flamenco style, neither the song nor the dance follows a prescribed script. They are never done exactly the same way twice and performers continue for as long as their emotions dictate and stamina allows.

The flamenco shows in Santa Cruz are for tourists but nonetheless good. In Triana it can be more authentic. In Calle Salado you can dance *sevillanas* – pacy folk dances. Purists would say you have to be in the right place at the right time for a spontaneous performance of the real thing.

Seville's James Bonds gather at the **Gran Casino Aljarafe** (🅰 Av. de la Arboleda in Tomares, just outside the city ☎ (902) 42 42 22 🔘 www.grancasinoaljarafe.com). Further away, by the seaside at Puerto de Santa María near Cádiz is the **Casino Bahía de Cádiz** (☎ (956) 87 10 42 🔘 www.casinobahiadecadiz.es).

If you fancy taking in a movie, most films screened in cinemas and on television are dubbed into Spanish, but you can often see original version ('VO') English-language films (with Spanish subtitles) at **Avenida 5 Cines** (🅰 C/ Marqués de Paradas 15 ☎ (954) 29 30 25).

Sport & relaxation

With its benign climate and abundance of green space, Seville is perfect for watching or taking part in outdoor activities. Its various parks are good places to stroll, run, cycle or rollerblade. Try the green strip beside the river starting near the Puente de Isabel II and continuing beyond the Plaza de Armas shopping centre (see page 87), and the extensive **Parque del Alamillo** (ⓦ www.parquedelalamillo.org) at the northern end of the Isla de Cartuja.

SPECTATOR SPORTS
Football
The city has two rival teams. FC Sevilla plays at the **Estadio Ramón Sánchez Pizjuán** (ⓐ C/ Sevilla Fútbol Club ⓣ (902) 410 011 ⓦ www.sevillafc.es), while Real Betis Balompié plays at the **Estadio Manuel Ruíz de Lopera** (ⓐ Av. Heliopolis ⓣ (954) 61 03 40 ⓦ www.realbetisbalompie.es), south of the city centre.

Bullfighting
Newcomers to Spain often don't know what to make of bullfighting, but then many Spaniards don't either. On TV and in the newspapers it's treated as a form of art combining the noblest elements of a spectator sport. Attending a bullfight is respectable almost to the point of being chic. On the other hand, it is easy to condemn *la corrida* as ritualised animal cruelty of the most cynical kind. Perhaps the only thing to do is see a bullfight for yourself and make up your own mind. As Seville has the most famous bullring in the country (see page 81), there is no better place to see what the fuss is about. The season runs from Easter to October with an important series of bullfights during the April Fair (see page 12).

🔺 *Make up your own mind about Spain's traditional national sport*

PARTICIPATION SPORTS
Golf
The 72-par course of the **Real Club de Golf de Sevilla** (ⓐ Autovía Sevilla-Utrera km 3, Alcalá de Guadaira ① (954) 12 43 01 ⓦ www.sevillagolf.com) is one of the best golf courses in Spain and has hosted the WGC World Cup as well as the 2010 Spanish Open.

RELAXATION
Turkish baths
Seville has two Turkish baths. The most convenient is **Aire de Sevilla** (ⓐ Aire 15 ① (955) 01 00 25 ⓦ www.airedesevilla.com ⓛ 10.00–22.00 Sun–Thur, 10.00–00.00 Fri & Sat), in the middle of Santa Cruz.
Medina Aljarafe (ⓐ Hernán Cortés 12, Bormujos ① (954) 78 83 44 ⓦ www.medinaaljarafe.com ⓛ 17.00–21.00 Wed, 11.00–21.00 Thur & Fri, 12.00–21.00 Sat, 12.00–19.00 Sun) is further out.

Accommodation

Seville offers a good choice of places to stay in all price ranges, which is unusual for large Spanish cities.

Hotels are officially ranked from 1 to 5 stars, but this doesn't tell you much except the quantity of facilities. Atmosphere and the standard of service do not always correspond to stars, and neither do prices. Seville's hotels – including almost all its boutique hotels in converted old houses – are concentrated in the picturesque and touristy Santa Cruz quarter (see page 60). This means that all the sights – and the best bars and restaurants – are within easy walking distance.

Generally cheaper are *hostales* (not to be confused with youth hostels), also known as *pensiones*. These are guesthouses that usually have en suite rooms but are unlikely to have 24-hour reception or room service and may not offer any meals apart from breakfast.

A well-kept family-run *pensión* or *hostal* can be a friendlier place to stay and often represents good value for money.

If you're really on a budget, consider camping. The tourist office (see page 152) can provide a list of suitable sites depending on how close to the city you wish to be.

HOTELS

Casa Sol y Luna £ Unusually for Seville, the Sol y Luna is a great-value *pensión*, with characterful rooms (though not all are en suite) in a converted mansion. ❸ C/ Pérez Galdós 1A (Santa Cruz & the city centre) ❶ (954) 21 06 82 ❿ www.casasolyluna1.com ❷ Bus: 10–12, 15, 20, 24, 27, 32

Hostal Sierpes £ A *hostal* in Santa Cruz that represents a good compromise between price and comforts. The en suite rooms

> **PRICE CATEGORIES**
> The price symbols indicate the approximate price of an
> en suite room for two people for one night in high season,
> including tax.
> £ up to €80 ££ €80–150 £££ over €150

surround a typical Andalucian patio. There is a café and restaurant and,
usefully for central Seville, a garage. ⓐ C/ Corral del Rey 22 (Santa Cruz
& the city centre) ⓣ (954) 22 49 48 ⓦ www.hsierpes.com Ⓝ Bus: C5

La Casa del Maestro ££ This city centre house was supposedly built in
1890 by a nobleman for one of his illegitimate children and was later
owned by flamenco guitarist Niño Ricardo. ⓐ C/ Niño Ricardo 5 (Santa
Cruz & the city centre) ⓣ (954) 50 00 07 ⓦ www.lacasadelmaestro.com
Ⓝ Bus: C5

Hostería del Laurel ££ A 22-room hotel and restaurant (see page 73)
in one of the picturesque squares at the heart of Santa Cruz. ⓐ Pl. de
los Venerables 5 (Santa Cruz & the city centre) ⓣ (954) 22 02 95
ⓦ www.hosteriadellaurel.com Ⓝ Bus: 1, 21, 23, C3, C4

Hotel Alcántara ££ A modernised 18th-century mansion with
21 guestrooms in the middle of Santa Cruz. ⓐ C/ Ximénez de
Enciso 28 (Santa Cruz & the city centre) ⓣ (954) 50 05 95
ⓦ www.hotelalcantara.net Ⓝ Bus: 1, 21, 23, C3–5

Hotel Alminar ££ A tiny, very friendly hotel close to La Giralda. Rooms
are simply but comfortably decorated, and excellent value for the price.

● *The Hostería del Laurel is in the heart of the Santa Cruz district*

@ C/ Álvarez Quintero 52 (Santa Cruz & the city centre) ❶ (954) 29 39 13
Ⓦ www.hotelalminar.com Ⓝ Tram: Archivo de Indias or Plaza Nueva;
bus: C5

Hotel Amadeus ££ A hotel by and for music lovers occupying an 18th-
century house. Each of the individually decorated 14 rooms is named
after a composer and concerts are held regularly. Upstairs there is
a terrace with views. @ C/ Farnesio 6 (Santa Cruz & the city centre)
❶ (954) 50 14 43 Ⓦ www.hotelamadeussevilla.com Ⓝ Bus: 1, 21, 23, C3–5

Hotel Goya ££ A clean, functional air-conditioned hotel with 19 rooms equipped with television and phone. ⓐ C/ Mateos Gago 31 (Santa Cruz & the city centre) ⓣ (954) 21 11 70 Ⓦ www.hotelgoyasevilla.com Ⓝ Bus: 1, 21, 23, C3–5

Hotel Murillo ££ Named after one of Seville's most famous painters and furnished in an old-fashioned style with armour and antiques, the Murillo has 14 one- or two-bedroom apartments equipped for self-catering. ⓐ Lope de Rueda 9 (Santa Cruz & the city centre) ⓣ (954) 21 60 95 Ⓦ www.hotelmurillo.com Ⓝ Bus: 1, 21, 23, C3, C4

Hotel Simón ££ An elegant but not overly formal old house in the centre of the city, just northwest of the cathedral. ⓐ C/ García de Vinuesa 19 (Santa Cruz & the city centre) ⓣ (954) 22 66 60 Ⓦ www.hotelsimonsevilla.com Ⓝ Bus: 5, 40, 41, C4, C5

Sacristía Santa Ana ££ A beautifully styled boutique hotel in the heart of the historic quarter. ⓐ Alameda de Hércules 22 (Beyond the centre) ⓣ (954) 91 57 22 Ⓦ www.hotelsacristia.com Ⓝ Bus: 13, 14

Petit Palace Santa Cruz ££–£££ Décor verges on the masculine, but rooms are centred around a porticoed patio in typically *sevillano* style. ⓐ C/ Muñoz y Pabón 18 (Santa Cruz & the city centre) ⓣ (954) 22 10 32 Ⓦ www.hthoteles.com Ⓝ Bus: C5

Alcoba del Rey de Sevilla £££ Neo-oriental boutique hotel near the Macarena basilica. And if you like anything you see in the hotel – even the beds, taps or floors – you can buy it and take it home with you. ⓐ C/ Bécquer 9 (Beyond the centre) ⓣ (954) 91 58 00 Ⓦ www.alcobadelrey.com Ⓝ Bus: 2, 10, 13, 14, C1–4

● *Top-class accommodation at the Hotel Alfonso XIII*

Casa Imperial £££ A converted 16th-century mansion near the Casa de Pilatos. ⓐ C/ Imperial 29 (Santa Cruz & the city centre) ① (954) 50 03 00 ⓦ www.casaimperial.com ⓝ Bus: 10–12, 15, 20, 24, 27, 32, C5, CC

Casa No 7 £££ An exquisitely decorated hotel just minutes from many of Seville's monuments. ⓐ C/ Vírgenes 7 (Santa Cruz & the city centre) ① (954) 22 15 81 ⓦ www.casanumero7.com ⓝ Bus: 10–12, 15, 20, 24, 27, 32, C5, CC

Las Casas del Rey de Baeza £££ An 18th-century mansion on a cobbled square in the centre, with a classical façade, a peaceful courtyard and a small, open-air pool on the roof. ⓐ Pl. Jesús de la Redención 2, off C/ Santiago (Santa Cruz & the city centre) ① (954) 56 14 96 ⓦ www.hospes.es ⓝ Bus: 10–12, 15, 20, 24, 27, 32, C5, CC

Convento La Gloria £££ Once a 15th-century convent, this is now a pretty boutique hotel, with many of the original features. It's a stone's throw from La Giralda, which some of its 35 rooms overlook. ⓐ C/ de Argote de Molina (Santa Cruz & the city centre) ⓘ (954) 29 36 70 Ⓝ Tram: Archivo de Indias; bus: C5

EME Catedral Hotel £££ On the doorstep of the cathedral, a chic hotel with four restaurants and a rooftop terrace and pool with cathedral views. ⓐ C/ Alemanes 27 (Santa Cruz & the city centre) ⓘ (954) 56 00 00 Ⓦ www.emecatedralhotel.com Ⓝ Tram: Archivo de Indias; bus: C5

Hotel Alfonso XIII £££ A classic luxury hotel with all the comforts its VIP guests could ask for, including a poolside bar and two restaurants (see page 78). ⓐ C/ San Fernando 2 (Beyond the centre) ⓘ (954) 91 70 00 Ⓦ www.hotel-alfonsoxiii.es Ⓝ Metro: Puerta de Jerez; tram: San Fernando

Taberna del Alabardero £££ This hotel northwest of the cathedral occupies the sensitively restored 19th-century house of a renowned Seville poet. It has seven comfortable rooms, each one of which is named after a different province of Andalucia. ⓐ C/ Zaragoza (Beyond the centre) ⓘ (954) 50 27 21 Ⓦ www.tabernadelalabardero.es Ⓝ Tram: Plaza Nueva

YOUTH HOSTELS
Oasis Backpackers Hostel £ A basic hotel in the city centre; breakfast is included. ⓐ Pl. de la Encarnación 29 (Santa Cruz & the city centre) ⓘ (954) 29 37 77 Ⓦ www.oasissevilla.com Ⓝ Bus: 10–12, 15, 16, 20, 24, 27, 32, C5, CC

THE BEST OF SEVILLE

Whether you are on a flying visit to Seville or taking a more leisurely break in southern Spain, here are some of the sights and activities you should try not to miss.

TOP 10 ATTRACTIONS

- **Barrio de Santa Cruz** A picture-postcard-pretty complex of streets and squares (see page 60)

- **Catedral y Giralda (Cathedral and the Giralda)** Two sights in one. The Giralda is essentially a topped-up minaret with a ramp leading all the way to the top. The tower makes a handy landmark to get your bearings. The massive Gothic cathedral below contains the tomb of (parts of) Christopher Columbus (see page 63)

- **Spring fiestas** Two very different celebrations fall close together, both of them spectacular. First come the processions of Holy Week (see page 8). Shortly afterwards comes the exuberant April Fair (see page 12)

- **Flamenco** The emblematic music and dance of southern Spain comes in many forms but is always performed with passion. There are plenty of places where you can see a show. And there is a museum to explain it (see page 68)

- **Museo de Bellas Artes (Museum of Fine Arts)** One of the great art galleries of Spain, concentrating on Seville's 'Golden Age' painters (see page 84)

- **Plaza de España** An extravagantly tiled monument in celebration of Spain in all its facets, this is the most prominent building in the leafy Parque de María Luisa, former showground of an international exhibition (see page 79)

- **Plaza de Toros de la Real Maestranza** The most famous bullring in the world. It's best to see it when packed out for a top *corrida*, but you can take a guided tour of it at any time (see page 81)

- **Real Alcázar** An exquisite royal palace built by the Christian kings of Castile in glorious Moorish style. The oldest occupied royal palace in Europe. It also has beautiful gardens (see page 66)

- **Río Guadalquivir** Seville wouldn't be Seville without its river, which is crossed by nine bridges. You can take a trip down it, stroll along its banks, or sit on a terrace of a bar or restaurant and take in a view of it at your leisure (see page 92)

- **Torre del Oro** There's not much to the short little 'Golden Tower' on the riverbank, but it's still a Seville landmark (see page 82)

🔵 *Courtyard view in the Real Alcázar*

Suggested itineraries

HALF-DAY: SEVILLE IN A HURRY

If you have only a morning or afternoon in Seville, there's no choice to make. Spend it in the Barrio de Santa Cruz (see page 60), but go up the Giralda Tower (see page 63) as well. If you're quick, you may be able to get around the Real Alcázar (see page 66), next door to the cathedral, as well. Santa Cruz has innumerable tapas bars and restaurants where you can grab a bite to eat to begin or end your visit.

1 DAY: TIME TO SEE A LITTLE MORE

With a whole day in Seville your best option is to stay in Santa Cruz and see the half-day itinerary at your leisure. You should also be able to stroll down to the riverside and see the bullring and Torre del Oro (see pages 81 and 82).

2–3 DAYS: TIME TO SEE MUCH MORE

One day will be spent as above, but the extra days will give you a chance to do more. Depending on your interest, you may choose to visit Triana (see page 95), the Museo de Bellas Artes (see page 84) or the Parque de María Luisa (see page 79). You could also take a day trip out of the city, perhaps to see Doñana National Park (see page 108) or even Córdoba.

LONGER: ENJOYING SEVILLE TO THE FULL

With a week or more you'll have time to fit in everything you want to see and do. If this is your first visit to southern Spain, try to get over to Granada for a day or two. You may want to spend another

NO8DO

Almost everywhere you go in Seville you'll see a symbol like some slick, inscrutable brand name carved on walls and written on posters: NO8DO.

Rather than a modern commercial invention it is a civic insignia that has been in use since the 13th century. Traditionally – and no one has yet come up with a better theory – it is held to be a mark of gratitude from King Alfonso X the Wise to the city for staying loyal to him during a struggle for the succession. It almost needs a competent texter to interpret it. The '8' stands for a skein of wool or *madeja* and so the message reads: *No-madeja-do* or *no me ha dejado* – that is, 'She [Seville] hasn't abandoned me.'

⬤ *How many of these can you spot around the city?*

Something for nothing

To see the best of Seville you don't have to spend money. You can enjoy its charm simply by strolling around its streets, squares and gardens. The Santa Cruz quarter is the obvious place to spend most time, but window shopping in the city centre also has its interest. If you've got time on your hands but no cash in your pockets, other good places to walk and see sights for free are the riverbanks and bridges of the Guadalquivir, Parque de María Luisa (especially the Plaza de España) and the former Expo 92 grounds on the Isla de Cartuja, which have a sort of postmodern fascination.

Plan ahead and you can see many of the city's essential monuments and museums without parting with a penny. Some of those that are not free all the time have a particular day of the week on which they waive the admission charge. The Archivo General de Indias (see page 68), Basílica de la Macarena (see page 76) and Hotel Alfonso XIII (see pages 39 & 78) are free all the time to everyone. The Museo de Bellas Artes (see page 84) and the Archaeological Museum (see page 84) are free to citizens of EU countries. The Centro Andaluz de Arte Contemporáneo (see page 98) on the Isla de Cartuja is free to EU citizens on Tuesdays (its grounds are free at any time), and the Torre del Oro (see page 82) and the Casa de Pilatos (Tuesday afternoons only, see page 62) are also free that day.

If you do your research well, you can turn the situation to your advantage and go in search of sights that other visitors might not bother with. La Macarena has several old churches, for instance, with vestiges of the mosques over which they were built. The Plaza de Armas shopping centre (see page 87) is the handsome old engine shed of a former railway station. Even in the middle of much transited Santa Cruz are three neglected Roman columns, immensely tall and rising out of a lush green pit in the ground on Calle Mármoles.

If you happen to be in Seville in spring, you will have all the street entertainment you want for free: first the semi-solemn semi-jubilant processions of Holy Week (see page 8); then the troops of colourfully dressed women heading on foot and in horse-drawn carriages for the showground of the April Fair (see page 12).

⬥ *Enjoy a stroll in the Parque de María Luisa*

When it rains

In summer, you'll probably be grateful for a little rain to cool things down. But at any other time of year, a few wet days can dampen your expectations of seeing a city in which sunshine and blue skies are the norm. Seville just isn't the same under brooding skies and it is as well to have a back-up plan to turn a disadvantage into a positive.

The obvious thing to do is take refuge in a museum such as the Museo de Bellas Artes (see page 84), Flamenco Museum (see page 68), Archaeological Museum (see page 84) or Palacio de Lebrija (see page 68). Similarly, the Archivo General de Indias (see page 68) and cathedral (see page 63) are also places you can get the best out of whatever the weather is doing. The Casa de Pilatos (see page 62), Real Alcázar (see page 66) and Centro Andaluz de Arte Contemporáneo (see page 98) offer at least something on a rainy day, although you won't see their outdoor spaces at their best.

Alternatively, you could forget sightseeing altogether and get down to some serious shopping. If you don't want to get wet hopping between shops it may be best to confine yourself to a department store such as El Corte Inglés (see page 69) or a shopping centre where you can keep dry as long as your money holds out. All have a good choice of bars and restaurants in which you can prolong your visit. The Plaza de Armas (see page 87) is the city's most convenient and pleasant shopping centre, but you may want somewhere larger – in which case head for Nervión Plaza (see page 87) which has a cinema next to it, or, further still, past Nervión Plaza, Los Arcos (see page 22).

Another option is to find yourself a pleasant bar (not hard to do in Seville) and either strike up a conversation with the locals or sit out the showers with a good book.

If you prefer to indulge yourself with physical pleasure while it pours down outside you can retreat into one of the city's Turkish baths (see page 33).

On a rainy evening when you feel like going out, try one of the flamenco shows in Santa Cruz or El Arenal.

🔺 *The Archivo General de Indias is a good bet if you're unlucky enough to get rain*

On arrival

Most visitors to Seville arrive at either the airport (a bus or taxi ride from the centre) or the railway station (just within walking distance). Either way, unless you already have a hotel to go to, the best thing to do is to make for the cathedral marked by the distinctive Giralda Tower and find your bearings there.

TIME DIFFERENCE
Spain follows Central European Time (CET), one hour ahead of Greenwich Mean Time. Between the end of March and the end of October clocks are put forward by one hour for Daylight Saving Time, on the same dates as in the UK.

ARRIVING
By air
National and international flights arrive at the **Aeropuerto de Sevilla** (☎ (954) 44 90 00 or (902) 40 47 04 ⓦ www.sevilla-airport.com or www.aena.es), otherwise known as San Pablo, 10 km (6 miles) northeast of the city. The quickest way to get into the city, depending on the traffic, is to take a taxi from an official rank. Regular buses between the city centre and the airport are run by **TUSSAM** (☎ (902) 45 99 54 ⓦ www.tussam.es); look out for line EA.

By rail
Seville's main railway station is **Estación de Santa Justa** (☎ (902) 43 23 43 ⓦ www.adif.es) on Avenida de Kansas City, a short bus ride or 20-minute walk east of the city centre. High-speed AVE trains from Madrid arrive here as well as trains from cities closer by including Jerez, Cádiz and Córdoba. There is a smaller railway station, San Bernardo,

● *Seville's main railway station, Santa Justa*

near the Prado de San Sebastián bus station. Spain's main rail operator is **RENFE** (🕿 (902) 32 03 20 🌐 www.renfe.es).

By road

If you arrive by coach you will be dropped off at one of the city's two bus stations. **Plaza de Armas** (🅐 Av. del Cristo de la Expiración 🕿 Station: (954) 90 77 37; bus info: (954) 90 80 40) serves western Spain and Madrid, while **Prado de San Sebastián** (🅐 C/ Manuel Vázquez Sagastizábal) serves most other destinations.

If you have to drive into Seville, it's best to have a secure parking place lined up and head straight for it. Avoid rush hour and driving in the twisting streets of Santa Cruz and La Macarena. If there is a quieter time to be driving in the city it is during the lunch break, around 15.00–16.00.

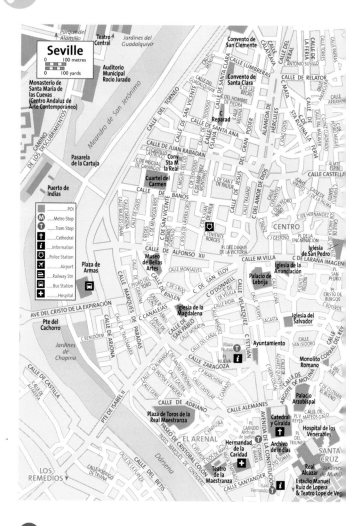

Seville

| | 0 | 100 metres |
| | 0 | 100 yards |

Parque del Alamillo

Teatro Central

Jardines del Guadalquivir

Convento de San Clemente

Convento de Santa Clara

CALLE LUMBRERAS

Auditorio Municipal Rocío Jurado

Monasterio de Santa María de las Cuevas (Centro Andaluz de Arte Contemporáneo)

Meandro de San Jerónimo

CALLE DEL TORNEO

C Reparad

CALLE DE SANTA ANA

ALAMEDA DE HÉRCULES

Pasarela de la Cartuja

CALLE DE JUAN RABADÁN

Conv Sta Mª la Real

Puerto de Indias

Cuartel del Carmen

CALLE DE BAÑOS

CALLE DEL AMOR DE DIOS

CENTRO

- POI
- Ⓜ Metro Stop
- Ⓣ Tram Stop
- ✝ Cathedral
- ⓘ Information
- Police Station
- ✈ Airport
- Railway Stn
- 🚌 Bus Station
- ✚ Hospital

Museo de Bellas Artes

CALLE DE ALFONSO XII

Iglesia de San Pedro

Iglesia de la Anunciación

Palacio de Lebrija

Plaza de Armas

C DE SAN ELOY

C O'DONNELL

Iglesia de la Magdalena

CALLE DE SAN PABLO

Iglesia del Salvador

AVE DEL CRISTO DE LA EXPIRACIÓN

Pte del Cachorro

Jardines de Chapina

Ayuntamiento

Monolito Romano

CALLE ZARAGOZA

Palacio Arzobispal

CALLE DE CASTILLA

PTE DE ISABEL II

CALLE DE ADRIANO

Plaza de Toros de la Real Maestranza

CALLE ALEMANES

Catedral y Giralda

Hospital de los Venerables

EL ARENAL

Hermandad de la Caridad

Archivo de Indias

SANTA CRUZ

Darsena

LOS REMEDIOS

Teatro de la Maestranza

CALLE SANTANDER

Real Alcázar

Jardines de Murillo

Estadio Manuel Ruiz de Lopera & Teatro Lope de Vega

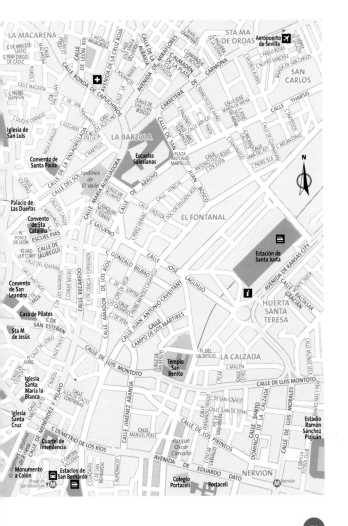

FINDING YOUR FEET

Seville is a lively, busy city and inevitably, like any big city, it has its criminals on the lookout for easy prey. That said, you should have no problems if you always keep your bag and camera close to you and don't stop in a dark alley to look at your map.

ORIENTATION

It's worth spending your first hour or so in the city becoming familiar with the layout, especially before you plunge into the labyrinthine streets of Santa Cruz. The cathedral and its Giralda Tower are always the main point of reference, and the river means you can never stray too far to the west. ❶ Note that many maps of Seville show the river running horizontally across them with east at the top, not north.

GETTING AROUND

The first line of Seville's shiny new **metro** (❶ (902) 364 985 Ⓦ www.metrodesevilla.org) opened in 2009, running from Cuidad Expo in the west, through the city centre via Puerta de Jerez and Gran Plaza, to Olivar de Quintos in the southeast. Trains run every few minutes from 06.30–23.00 Monday to Thursday, 06.30–02.00 Friday and Saturday and 07.30–23.00 on Sunday. Lines 2, 3, 4 are still under construction.

You can buy individual tickets at metro stations but it is better value to obtain a multi-trip *Tarjeta Multiviaje*, available from *estancos* (tobacconists), street kiosks, metro stations and tram stops. The card costs €1.50 and you must buy a minimum of ten trips; these are then deducted from your card as you travel and can be topped up by cash or credit card. You can use the *Tarjeta Multiviaje* on the metro, tram and bus systems. An alternative option is the *Tarjeta Turística*

IF YOU GET LOST, TRY ...

Excuse me, do you speak English?
Perdone, ¿habla usted inglés?
Perdoneh, ¿ahbla oosted eengless?

Excuse me, is this the right way to the Old Town/the city centre/the tourist office/the station/the bus station?
Perdone, ¿por aquí se va al casco antiguo/al centro de la ciudad/a la oficina de turísmo/a la estación de trenes/a la estación de autobuses?
Perdoneh, ¿por akee seh ba al kasko anteegwo/al thentroe dey la theeoodad/a la offeetheena dey toorismoe/a la estatheeon dey treness/a la estatheeon dey owtoebooses?

Can you point to it on my map?
¿Puede señalármelo en el mapa?
¿Pwaydeh senyalarmayloe en el mapa?

(tourist card), valid for unlimited transport for one or three days.

As well as the metro, there is a modern street-level *tranvía* (tram) known as **Metrocentro** (☎ (902) 45 05 50 🌐 www.tussam.es), which has stops at Plaza Nueva, Archivo de Indias, Puerta de Jerez and the Prado de San Sebastián bus station. An extension to Santa Justa station is planned. Trams run 07.30–01.30 daily.

Buses are generally efficient. Pay the driver or use the *Tarjeta Multiviaje* or *Tarjeta Turística*. For information, call ☎ (900) 85 55 58 or check 🌐 www.tussam.es or www.consorciotransportes-sevilla.com.

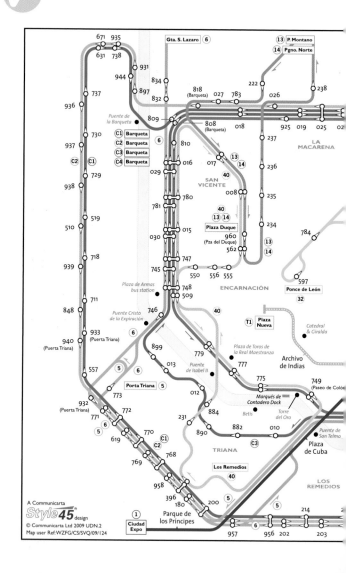

A Communicarta
Style 45 design
© Communicarta Ltd 2009 UDN.2
Map user Ref:WZFG/CS/SVQ/09/124

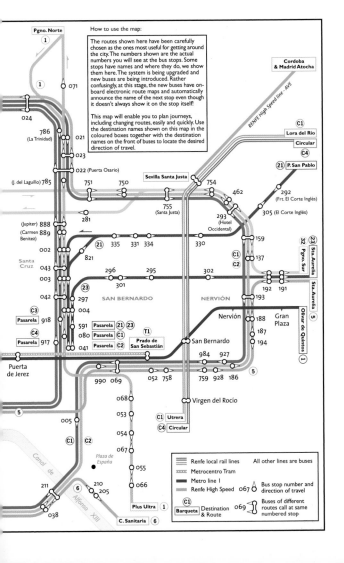

How to use the map:

The routes shown here have been carefully chosen as the ones most useful for getting around the city. The numbers shown are the actual numbers you will see at the bus stops. Some stops have names and where they do, we show them here. The system is being upgraded and new buses are being introduced. Rather confusingly, at this stage, the new buses have on-board electronic route maps and automatically announce the name of the next stop even though it doesn't always show it on the stop itself!

This map will enable you to plan journeys, including changing routes, easily and quickly. Use the destination names shown in the coloured boxes together with the destination names on the front of buses to locate the desired direction of travel.

Pgno. Norte

Cordoba & Madrid Atocha

RENFE High Speed line - AVE

024

786 (La Trinidad)

071

021

023

022 (Puerta Osario)

(J. del Laguillo) 785

751   750

755 (Santa Justa)

281

Sevilla Santa Justa

754

462

292 (Frt. El Corte Inglés)

305 (El Corte Inglés)

293 (Hotel Occidental)

C1 Lora del Rio
Circular
C4
21 P. San Pablo

(Jupiter) 888
(Carmen Benitez) 889

002

821

335   331 334

330

159

137

C1
C2

32 Pgno. Sur

23 Sta. Aurelia

Santa Cruz

043

003

042

297

296   295

301

302

192 191

193

Sta. Aurelia

5

SAN BERNARDO

NERVIÓN

004

C3 Pasarela
918

591 Pasarela 21 23
080 Pasarela C1
917 Pasarela C2

C4 Pasarela

T1
Prado de San Sebastián

Nervión

188

187

194

Gran Plaza

Olivar de Quintos

1

San Bernardo

041

Puerta de Jerez

990 069

052 758

984 927

759 928 186

5

068

Virgen del Rocío

005

053

C1 Utrera
C4 Circular

C1   C2

054

067

Plaza de España

055

066

211

6

210
205

Plus Ultra   1

038

Canal de

Alfonso XIII

C. Sanitaria   6

Renfe local rail lines   All other lines are buses
Metrocentro Tram
Metro line 1
Renfe High Speed   067 ⋀ Bus stop number and direction of travel
C1 Barqueta Destination & Route   069 Buses of different routes call at same numbered stop

SEVILLE CARD

The Seville Card gives free admission for one, two or three days to all the major monuments and museums in the city (sometimes with guided tour), Isla Mágica and the zoo. You can use either of the official tour buses (see below), take a cruise down the river and, if you pay a little more, have unlimited use of the TUSSAM public bus network. Show the card and you'll get discounts in many restaurants, shops, flamenco shows and clubs. ☎ (902) 08 89 08 ⓦ www.sevillacard.es

A good way to see a lot in a hurry is to take an open-top double-decker tour bus ride with either **SevillaTour** (☎ (902) 10 10 81 ⓦ www.sevillatour.com ⏱ 10.00–18.00 Nov–Mar; 10.00–22.00 Apr–Oct) or **Sevirama Tour** (☎ (954) 56 06 93 ⓦ www.busturistico.com ⏱ 10.00–18.00 Nov–Apr; 10.00–22.00 May–Oct). You can catch them near the Torre del Oro and hop on or hop off at most of the principal sights around the city.

Taxis are easily hailed on any main street and not too costly. For a pick-up call **Radio Taxi** (☎ (954) 58 00 00) or **Tele Taxi** (☎ (954) 62 22 22). A green light means a taxi is for hire. The fare will be fixed by meter, which may start at a minimum charge. Tariffs increase at night and if you have luggage.

With no hills, around 100 km (60 miles) of cycle lanes and a municipal bike-hire system, Seville is a good city to cycle around. The **SEVici** bike hire service (☎ (902) 01 10 32 ⓦ www.sevici.es) allows you to hire a bicycle for a maximum of one week from numerous bike service stations around the city. You need to authorise a €150 returnable deposit on your credit card. A weekly pass costs €5, allowing you to hire bikes at the rate of one euro per hour (the first half hour is free). You can return them at any SEVici station.

Cyclotour (📞 (954) 686 666 🌐 www.cyclotour.es) is a fun way of exploring the reaches of Parque de María Luisa or beyond. The three- or six-person four-wheel cycles can be hired from the stand at Avenida de Hernán Cortés in Parque Maria Luisa, by Plaza de España, from 10.00 each morning.

Seville looks different from the river as the traffic noise recedes and you sail under its various bridges. Cruises are operated by **Cruceros Torre del Oro** (📍 Alcalde Marqués de Contadero, next to the Torre del Oro 📞 (954) 56 16 92 🌐 www.crucerostorredeloro.com). Boats leave every 30 minutes (🕐 10.00–23.00 May–Oct; 10.00–19.00

🔺 *Take a taxi from the station – otherwise it's more fun to walk*

HORSE-DRAWN CARRIAGES

These exist, of course, purely for tourists but, come the April Fair (see page 12), anyone who is anyone in Seville will be seen driving around Seville at horse-pace. And it is an undeniably leisurely and enjoyable way to get the flavour of the city. ❷ Drivers wait for fares in the Plaza del Triunfo outside the cathedral, in the Parque de María Luisa (next to the Plaza de España) and near the Torre del Oro

Nov–Apr) for a one-hour trip to see the historical and modern sights of the city. At weekends from May to September they also sail down to the mouth of the Guadalquivir at Sanlúcar de Barrameda on the edge of Doñana National Park (see page 108).

CAR HIRE

Narrow streets and traffic jams mean it's not worth trying to drive around the city centre. In addition, car parks and parking spaces can be hard to find. If you have arrived by car it is best to leave it parked in a hotel garage or secure car park and explore on foot, public transport or taxi. Three of the most reputable companies who have offices in the city are:

Avis ❶ (902) 13 55 31 Ⓦ www.avis.es

Hertz ❶ (902) 40 24 05 Ⓦ www.hertz.es

National/Atesa ❶ (954) 51 47 35 Ⓦ www.atesa.es

For more information on driving, see page 143.

---

❶ *Aerial view of Seville with her famous bullring*

THE CITY OF
Seville

Santa Cruz & the city centre

The Barrio de Santa Cruz is the heart and soul of Seville. Indeed if all the allures of southern Spain could be distilled into one neighbourhood of one city, this tangle of picturesque streets, squares and beguiling alleyways would definitely be it.

In many ways, the area is a seamless blend of the authentic and the stereotypical: white houses with details picked out in ochre and crimson, the forbidding iron grilles over their windows offset by pots of flowering geraniums. At every turn there is some pleasant bar or restaurant with outdoor tables ready for breakfast, tapas or a leisurely meal. The main reason why Santa Cruz has survived quite as intact as it has is that there are few streets through it built for cars. The best (but busiest) pedestrian route into Santa Cruz is through the short tunnel in the corner of Patio de Banderas (next to the exit from the Real Alcázar, see page 66), which leads into Calle Judería, whose name is a reminder that this was once the Jewish quarter of the city.

Santa Cruz proper stretches east from here to Calle de Menéndez y Pelayo – this is its picture-postcard core – but it continues northwards to the Casa de Pilatos. Once you are immersed in the labyrinth, a map is not much use, but there are two landmarks to help you. Occasionally you'll catch a glimpse of the Giralda (see page 63), giving you a rough west point; to the south the *barrio* is limited by the gardens of the Real Alcázar.

Beautiful though it is, after a while Santa Cruz can feel a little claustrophobic. So it can be a relief to discover Seville's agreeable city centre, helpfully known simply as 'Centro'. To reach the Barrio de Santa Cruz, take the metro to Puerta de Jerez or the tram to San Fernando or Archivo de Indias. To reach the shopping streets of the city centre, catch the tram to Plaza Nueva.

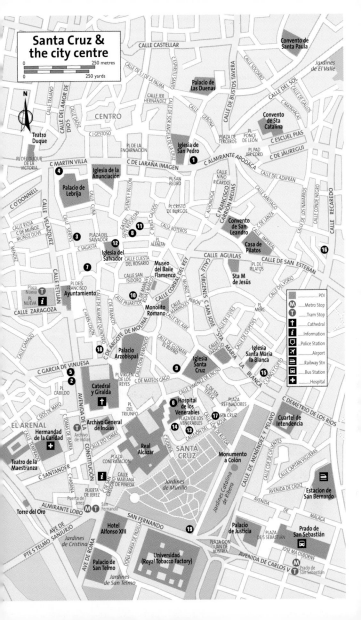

Santa Cruz & the city centre

0 _____ 250 metres
0 _____ 250 yards

N

CENTRO

Teatro Duque

Convento de Santa Paula

Jardines de El Valle

Palacio de Las Duenas

Convento de Sta Catalina

CALLE CASTELLAR

CALLE DE S.J. DE LA PALMA

CALLE DE BUSTOS TAVERA

CALLE DEL SOL

CALLE DE GALLOS

CALLE MATAHACAS

C J GESTOSO

CALLE ESCUEL PIAS

C DE JÁUREGUI

C DE LARAÑA IMAGEN

Iglesia de San Pedro **1**

PL DE LA ENCARNACIÓN

C MARTIN VILLA **4**

Iglesia de la Anunciación

Palacio de Lebrija

3

PLAZA DEL SALVADOR **8** **11** **12**

7 Iglesia del Salvador

CALLE CUESTA DEL ROSARIO

Museo del Baile Flamenco

10

Monolito Romano

Ayuntamiento

PL DEL DUQUE DE LA VICTORIA

PL SAN PEDRO

PL CRISTO DE BURGOS

PL ALFALFA

PL DE TERCEROS

PL PONCE DE LEÓN

CALLE DEL AZAFRÁN

Convento de San Leandro

Casa de Pilatos

PL DE PILATOS

16

CALLE AGUILAS

Sta M de Jesús

Palacio Arzobispal **18**

Catedral y Giralda **+**

Archivo General de Indias

Real Alcázar

Iglesia Santa Cruz **9**

Hospital de los Venerables **6** **17**

PLAZA DE LOS VENERABLES **14** **13**

Iglesia Santa Maria la Blanca **15**

EL ARENAL

Hermandad de la Caridad **+**

Teatro de la Maestranza

Torre del Oro

Jardines de Cristina

Palacio de San Telmo

Jardines de San Telmo

Hotel Alfonso XIII

Jardines de Murillo

Universidad (Royal Tobacco Factory)

19

Monumento a Colón

Cuartel de Intendencia

Palacio de Justicia

Prado de San Sebastián

Estacion de San Bernardo

	POI
Ⓜ	Metro Stop
Ⓣ	Tram Stop
✝	Cathedral
ⓘ	Information
	Police Station
✈	Airport
	Railway Stn
	Bus Station
✚	Hospital

SIGHTS & ATTRACTIONS

Casa de Pilatos

This aristocratic palace dates from the late 15th and early 16th centuries and speaks of Seville at its most wealthy and powerful. It was named 'the House of Pontius Pilate' after one of its early owners, Don Fadrique, the first Marquis of Tarifa, returned from the Holy Land in 1519 and discovered that the distance between it and a local shrine was the same as that between the supposed site of the Praetorium (where Christ was condemned to death) in Jerusalem and Golgotha (where he was crucified).

The house, owned by the Dukes of Medinaceli and administered

◆ *The tranquil, shady gardens of the Casa de Pilatos*

on their behalf by a foundation, is in a mixture of Gothic, Mudéjar (derived from Islamic architecture) and Italian Renaissance styles. It has a number of interesting decorative features including coffered ceilings, paintings, furniture, classical statues, frescoes and a marvellous dome over the main staircase. The walls around the two-storey central patio are worth seeing (even if you ignore the rest of the building), as they are covered with old tiles in a glorious clash of colours and styles. Outside, the Renaissance gardens are worth seeing, too.

ⓐ Pl. de Pilatos 1 ① (954) 22 52 98 ⓦ www.fundacionmedinaceli.org ⓛ 09.00–18.00 Nov–Mar; 09.00–19.00 Apr–Oct; guided tours every half hour from 10.00 ⓝ Bus: 10, 11, 12, 15, 20, 24, 27, 32, C5, CC. Admission charge (free from 13.00 Tues for EU citizens)

Catedral y Giralda (Cathedral & Giralda Tower)

'We'll build a church that will make anyone who looks at it think we were mad,' the city fathers are supposed to have said in the early 14th century as they set out to build Seville's great cathedral. The building took over a century to complete and the result was, and is, the largest Gothic building in Europe.

It stands on the site of a 12th-century mosque, and the only surviving remains of the original building are the cloister of the Patio de los Naranjos ('Courtyard of the Orange Trees', which was used for ritual ablutions by Muslim worshippers) and the Giralda Tower, formerly a minaret, which looms above the cathedral as the city's unmistakable landmark.

Inside, five aisles divided into nine sections each, and flanked by 20 chapels, create a massive floor space. The focal point is inevitably the high altar with its great altarpiece, one of the largest in the world, made of gold panels carved in relief by Flemish and Spanish artists. Other features to look out for are the Royal Chapel, the

◆ *The Giralda Tower soars over Seville's massive Gothic cathedral*

138 stained-glass windows and the ornate tomb of at least some of Christopher Columbus (see opposite).

The highlight of the visit, however, is a climb up the 104 m (341 ft) Giralda Tower. The tower has a series of ramps running up the middle of it which once allowed horses or mules to be ridden to the top.

The tower is actually an ingenious bit of architectural grafting as it is one tower superimposed on another. The bottom two-thirds are a brick-built minaret; the upper part is a stone-and-brick Renaissance belfry added in 1568. On the pinnacle of the spire stands a weathervane: a bronze figure of Faith popularly known as 'El Giraldillo' from which

THE MYSTERY OF COLUMBUS'S TOMB

Christopher Columbus has travelled almost as much since he's been dead as he did when he was alive. When he handed in his passport for good (or so you might reasonably have thought), in Valladolid on 20 May 1506, he was initially buried in a cemetery in the city. But three years later his family had the corpse taken to Seville where his eldest son, Diego, was buried beside him in 1526. Seville was, of course, of great significance to Columbus, as it was from here that he set off on the journey that would eventually lead him to America. But Diego's widow insisted on having both bodies moved to Santo Domingo on the Caribbean island of Hispaniola, claiming that that's what Christopher would have wanted. But his resting in peace here was disturbed by international events. When the French threatened to capture Hispaniola in 1795, a worried Spain had his remains transferred for safe keeping to Havana, Cuba. A century later, Cuba gained its independence and Columbus was again relocated to his final resting place in Seville cathedral.

Or was he? Rumours have abounded for years that Christopher never actually made it back to Seville. Certainly, each time he was moved (or was supposed to have been), there was the possibility of an embarrassing mistake being made, and there is some evidence that it was the body of Diego that was (erroneously) moved to Havana. This would have meant that Christopher Columbus stayed buried in Santo Domingo in the Dominican Republic. However, DNA tests in 2006 proved that at least some of Columbus's remains are in the tomb in Seville. Some? So where's the rest of him?

the tower derives its name. ⓐ Av. de la Constitución (entrance off Pl. Virgen de los Reyes) ⓘ (954) 21 49 71 ⓦ www.catedraldesevilla.es ⓛ 11.00–17.00 Mon–Sat, 14.30–18.00 Sun, Sept–June; 09.30–16.00 Mon–Sat, 14.30–18.00 Sun, July & Aug ⓜ Tram: Archivo de Indias. Admission charge

Real Alcázar (Royal Alcazar)

What makes this royal pad (the King stays here when he's in town) special is the way in which Muslim architectural styles have been fused with Christian ones. The core of the Alcázar is the Mudéjar Palace (also called the Palacio de Don Pedro), which was created by Pedro I (the Cruel) between 1364 and 1366. To fulfil his plans he sent to Córdoba and Granada for the best Muslim craftsmen working in his day.

The complex is entered by the Puerta del León, which leads into the Patio del León. One room to the left is the Patio del Yeso (Patio of the Plaster), the only bit of the Almohad Palace still intact.

From the Patio del León you step into the Patio de la Montería, the fulcrum of the complex where the court used to assemble for hunting expeditions. Directly in front of you is the façade of the Mudéjar Palace. But before you enter it, have a look at the audience chamber, or Casa de Contratación, to the right. Against one wall here is the *Altarpiece of the Navigators*, painted in 1531–6 and almost certainly the first work of art to depict the discovery of the Americas. In its central panel the Virgin Mary spreads her cape protectively over an assembly of discoverers and *conquistadores*.

The finest room of the palace is the Salón de los Embajadores (Hall of the Ambassadors), which is noticeable for its great dome – a complex geometric arrangement of interlocking gold-painted wood.

Also worth seeing are the Patio de las Muñecas (Patio of the Dolls) named after the two small faces that adorn one of its arches,

● *Moorish designs in the courtyard of the Real Alcázar*

and the Patio de las Doncellas (Patio of the Maidens), with its superb plasterwork. North of the Mudéjar Palace you pass into the Salones de Carlos V, sumptuous, Gothic-vaulted apartments and a chapel added on the orders of the eponymous monarch. Behind the palace is a large triangle of delightful walled gardens. ⓐ Pl. del Triunfo ① (954) 50 23 23 Ⓦ www.patronato-alcazarsevilla.es ● 09.30–19.00 Apr–Sept; 09.30–17.00 Oct–Mar Ⓝ Tram: Archivo de Indias. Admission charge

CULTURE

Archivo General de Indias (General Archive of the Indies)

This immense depository of the records of imperial Spain's centuries of colonialism occupies a 16th-century building. In the 18th century King Carlos III decided to use it to archive in one place the vast store of documents relating to Spain's New World possessions. It is still a working library consulted by scholars from all over the world. Its 8 km (5 miles) of shelves hold 43,000 files and more than 80 million pages of original documents – including Columbus's journal. ⓐ Av. de la Constitución 3 ① (954) 21 12 34 ⓦ www.mcu.es ⓛ 09.30–16.45 Mon–Sat, 10.00–13.45 Sun ⓝ Tram: Archivo de Indias

Museo del Baile Flamenco (Flamenco Museum)

This museum aims to present flamenco as a mainstream art form. There's a gift shop selling various flamenco-related items, plus evening concerts. If you are here for long enough, you can even take flamenco dance classes. ⓐ C/ Manuel Rojas Marcos 3, near Pl. Alfalfa ① (954) 34 03 11 ⓦ www.museoflamenco.com ⓛ 09.30–19.00 (last entry 18.30) ⓝ Bus: C5. Admission charge

Palacio de Lebrija (Palace of Lebrija)

This 16th-century Renaissance-Mudéjar palace could be considered the city's alternative archaeological museum. Among many other items is one of the finest mosaics from the Roman remains of Itálica (see page 108). Upstairs are the living quarters of the Countess after whom the palace is named. ⓐ C/ Cuna 8 ① (954) 22 78 02 ⓦ www.palaciodelebrija.com ⓛ 10.30–19.30 Mon–Fri, 10.00–14.00, 16.00–18.00 Sat, 10.00–14.00 Sun, Sept–June; 09.00–15.00 Mon–Fri, 10.00–14.00 Sat, July & Aug ⓝ Bus: 13, 14, 40, C5, CC. Admission charge

RETAIL THERAPY

Seville's best shops are concentrated along Calle Sierpes and Calle Tetuán, which turns into Calle Velázquez as it heads north towards Plaza del Duque de la Victoria.

Adolfo Domínguez Spanish designer known especially for his men's suits and shoes. ⓐ C/ Sierpes 2 ⓣ (954) 21 30 67 ⓦ www.adolfodominguez.es ⓛ 10.00–20.30 Mon–Sat ⓝ Bus: 13, 14, 40

La Alacena Real Old grocer's-cum-delicatessen selling fine wines, olive oils, cheeses, hams and other fine Spanish foods. Any product can be vacuum packed on the premises for safe transport home. ⓐ C/ Pajaritos 11 ⓣ (954) 22 00 90 ⓛ 11.00–15.00, 18.00–22.00 Mon–Fri ⓝ Bus: C5

Casa Rodriguez Statues of saints, icons and sundry religious objects. ⓐ C/ de Francos 35 ⓣ (954) 22 78 42 ⓛ 10.00–13.30, 17.00–20.30 Mon–Fri, 10.00–14.00 Sat ⓝ Bus: C5

Compás Sur Mainly a place to buy recordings of flamenco, this shop will also set you up with flamenco guitar or dance classes. ⓐ C/ Cuesta del Rosario 7E, between Pl. Alfalfa & Pl. del Salvador ⓣ (954) 21 56 62 ⓦ www.compas-sur.com ⓛ 10.30–14.00, 17.30–21.00 Mon–Fri, 11.00–14.00, 17.00- 20.00 Sat ⓝ Bus: C5

El Corte Inglés Spain's leading department store, on eight floors with a restaurant and supermarket stocked with delicacies. ⓐ Pl. del Duque de la Victoria 8 ⓣ (954) 59 70 00 ⓦ www.elcorteingles.es ⓛ 10.00–22.00 Mon–Sat ⓝ Bus: 13, 14, 40

Feliciano Foronda Beautiful handmade shawls in the finest silk, including *mantillas* (see page 23). There are a variety of styles to choose from, all authentically Spanish. ⓐ C/ Álvarez Quintero 44 ❶ (954) 22 91 48 ⓛ 09.30–13.30, 17.00–20.00 Mon–Fri, 09.30–13.30 Sat Ⓝ Tram: Plaza Nueva

○ *Explore the narrow shopping streets near the cathedral*

Sevillarte A ceramics and handicraft centre selling traditional and new designs. Also stocks Lladró porcelain (made in Valencia). ⓐ C/ Sierpes 66 ① (954) 21 28 36 ⓦ www.sevillarte.com ① 10.00–18.00 Mon–Fri, 10.00–14.00 Sat (occasionally open 10.00–13.00 Sun) ⓝ Bus: 13, 14, 40

Victorio y Lucchino A world-renowned fashion duo who started their business in Seville in the 1970s and are still based here. Their bold and colourful designs have an unmistakeably Andaluz feel. ⓐ Pl. Nueva 10 ① (954) 50 26 60 ⓦ www.victorioylucchino.com ① 10.00–14.00, 17.00–20.30 Mon–Sat ⓝ Tram: Plaza Nueva

TAKING A BREAK

CAFÉS & ICE CREAMS
Heladería Rayas £ ❶ Seville's most renowned ice cream shop, with a range of wonderful homemade flavours, from gazpacho to olive oil. ⓐ C/ Almirante Apodaca 1, near Pl. San Pedro ① (954) 22 17 46 ① 15.00–22.00 or 23.00 ⓝ Bus: 10–12, 15, 16, 20, 24, 27, 32, C5

Horno San Buenaventura £ ❷ One of the only cafés in Seville that uses fresh (rather than long-life) milk – hence it's known for serving the best coffee in town. With a bakery as well as café tables, it's a great place for breakfast. ⓐ Corner Av. de la Constitución & C/ Garcia de Vinuesa ① (954) 22 18 19 ① 07.30–23.00 Mon–Sat, 09.00–23.00 Sun ⓝ Tram: Archivo de Indias

Ochoa £ ❸ An old cake shop and tea room which serves homemade ice creams and claims to serve the best milkshakes in Seville. ⓐ C/ Sierpes 45 ① (954) 22 55 28 ① 10.00–21.00 ⓝ Bus: C5

Confitería La Campana ££ ❹ Seville's oldest café-cum-cake shop: a
landmark on the square of the same name at the end of Calle Sierpes.
🅐 C/ Sierpes 1–3 ☎ (954) 22 35 70 🆆 www.confiterialacampana.com
🕐 08.00–22.00 Mon–Fri, 08.00–23.00 Sat & Sun Ⓝ Bus: 13, 14, 40, C5, CC

TAPAS & BARS

Casa Morales £ ❺ The city's second-oldest bar, and a good place to
eat tapas and taste wines. 🅐 C/ García de Vinuesa 11 ☎ (954) 22 12 42
🕐 12.00–16.00, 20.00–00.00 Ⓝ Tram: Archivo de Indias

Casa Román £ ❻ A dusty local bar, with great tapas and tables
outside in a peaceful, sunny square. The speciality is excellent *jamón
ibérico*. 🅐 Pl. de los Venerables 1 ☎ (954) 22 84 83 🕐 09.00–16.00,
19.30–00.00 Mon–Sat, 11.00–16.00 Sun Ⓝ Bus: 1, 21, 23, C3, C4

Entrecárceles £ ❼ Sophisticated, award-winning tapas are served
with a variety of vintage wines and sherries in this handsome little
bar. 🅐 C/ Faisanes 1, off Pl. San Francisco 🕐 12.00–16.00, 19.00–00.00
Ⓝ Tram: Plaza Nueva

Europa £ ❽ Come here for tapas at any time of day or an early
breakfast that's hearty and good value. 🅐 C/ Siete Revueltas 35
☎ (954) 21 79 08 🆆 www.bareuropa.info 🕐 08.00–01.00 Ⓝ Bus: C5

Cervecería Giralda ££ ❾ Exquisite tapas including mushroom and
cod pie, stuffed courgettes, sirloin stuffed with ham, egg and parsley,
and 'Seville's most famous stuffed peppers'. 🅐 C/ Mateos Gago 1
☎ (954) 22 82 50 🕐 09.00–00.00 Mon–Sat, 10.00–00.00 Sun
Ⓝ Bus: 1, 21, 23, C3–5

La Estrella ££ ❿ Long-standing bar famed for its award-winning aubergine covered with fried tomatoes, peppers, onions, chopped prawns, hard boiled egg and bechamel sauce and served *au gratin*. ⓐ C/ Estrella 3, off C/ de Argote de Molina ❶ (954) 21 93 25 ❷ 09.00–00.00 Mon–Sat ❷ Bus: C5

AFTER DARK

RESTAURANTS

La Habanita £ ⓫ Cuban food including vegan and vegetarian options. ⓐ C/ Golfo 3, near Pl. Alfalfa ❶ (954) 22 02 02 ❷ www.habanita.es ❷ 12.30–16.30, 20.00–23.00 Mon–Fri, 12.30–16.30, 20.00–00.00 Sat, 12.30–16.30 Sun ❷ Bus: C5

La Alicantina ££ ⓬ Bar and restaurant in which the menu is especially strong on fish and seafood. Large terrace. Vegetarians catered for. ⓐ Pl. del Salvador 2 ❶ (954) 22 61 22 ❷ 10.00–00.00 ❷ Bus: C5

Corral del Agua ££ ⓭ Despite its position in the heart of touristville, Corral del Agua maintains its high standards of local cooking. Ask for a table on its leafy patio, where a fountain gurgles gently. ⓐ Callejón del Agua 6 ❶ (954) 22 48 41 ❷ 12.30–16.00, 20.00–00.00 ❷ Bus: 1, 21, 23, C3, C4

Hostería del Laurel ££ ⓮ Supposedly the place where Zorillo was inspired to write *Don Juan Tenorio*. A good place for tapas or a full meal at outdoor tables in one of Santa Cruz's picturesque squares. Also a hotel (see page 35). ⓐ Pl. de los Venerables 5 ❶ (954) 22 02 95 ❷ www.hosteriadellaurel.com ❷ 11.00–16.00, 20.00–00.00 ❷ Bus: 1, 21, 23, C3, C4

La Judería ££ ⓯ Highly rated restaurant for a special lunch or night out. Traditional Andalucian cuisine and a large selection of wines. ⓐ C/ Cano y Cueto 13 ⓣ (954) 42 64 56 ⓦ www.modestorestaurantes.com ⓛ 13.00–17.00, 19.30–00.30 Ⓝ Bus: 1, 21, 23, C3, C4

Restaurante Becerríta ££–£££ ⓰ Sevillian cuisine and tapas. ⓐ C/ Recaredo 9 ⓣ (954) 41 20 57 ⓦ www.becerrita.com ⓛ 12.30–16.30, 20.00–00.30 Mon–Sat, 12.30–16.30 Sun Ⓝ Bus: 1, 21, 23, C3, C4

La Albahaca £££ ⓱ Atmospheric and elegant restaurant in a beautiful old 1920s house. ⓐ Pl. Santa Cruz 12 ⓣ (954) 22 07 14 ⓦ www.andalunet.com/la-albahaca ⓛ 12.00–16.00, 20.00–00.00 Mon–Sat (occasionally open Sun in summer) Ⓝ Bus: 1, 21, 23, C3, C4

Casa Robles £££ ⓲ A chain of four establishments, including a tapas bar. ⓐ C/ Álvarez Quintero 58 ⓣ (954) 21 31 50 ⓦ www.roblesrestaurantes.com ⓛ 13.00–01.00 Ⓝ Tram: Plaza Nueva; bus: C5

Restaurante Egaña Oriza £££ ⓳ Usually classed as Seville's top restaurant. The cuisine is a fusion of Basque and Andalucian. ⓐ C/ San Fernando 41 ⓣ (954) 22 72 54 ⓛ 13.30–15.30, 20.30–23.30 Tues–Sat, 13.30–15.30 Sun Ⓝ Metro: Puerta de Jerez; tram: San Fernando

FLAMENCO SHOWS

Auditorio Álvarez Quintero A fun flamenco venue close to the cathedral. ⓐ C/ Álvarez Quintero 48 ⓣ (954) 29 39 49 ⓦ www.alvarezquintero.com ⓛ From 20.30 Ⓝ Tram: Plaza Nueva; bus: C5

La Carbonería This bar in the premises of a former coal merchant is a well-known place to hear and see flamenco. ⓐ C/ de Levies 18

**(954) 21 44 60 or 22 99 45 ⏰ 20.00–02.00 🚌 Bus: 1, 21, 23, C3, C4

Casa de la Memoria A well-respected centre for the study of Andalucian culture. 🏠 C/ Ximénez de Enciso **(954) 56 06 70 🌐 www.casadelamemoria.es ⏰ Shows: 21.00; sometimes also 19.30 & 22.30 🚌 Bus: 1, 21, 23, C3–5

Los Gallos Claims to keep it simple and authentic. 🏠 Pl. de Santa Cruz 11 **(954) 21 69 81 🌐 www.tablaolosgallos.com ⏰ Shows: 20.00 & 22.30 ❗ Advance booking recommended (online tickets available) 🚌 Bus: 1, 21, 23, C3, C4

Museo del Baile Flamenco (Flamenco Museum) The world's only flamenco museum (see page 68) offers daily live performances in its covered patio. 🏠 C/ Manuel Rojas Marcos 3, near Pl. Alfalfa **(954) 34 03 11 🌐 www.museoflamenco.com ⏰ Shows: 19.00 Mon–Thur, 19.30 Fri & Sat 🚌 Bus: C5

CLUBS & BARS

Catedral One of the few clubs in the city centre, this one plays on a religious theme. The music is mainly hip hop, house and R&B. 🏠 C/ Cuesta del Rosario 12 **(954) 21 90 29 ⏰ 16.00–01.00 Mon–Wed, 16.00–03.00 Thur–Sun 🚌 Bus: C5

Santo Terraza It must be the best view from any bar in Seville – the terrace looks right over the Giralda Tower. The drinks are as sophisticated as the décor, and there's a restaurant inside if you want to stay put. 🏠 C/ Alemanes 27 **(954) 56 00 00 🌐 www.emecatedralhotel.com ⏰ 20.00–02.00 May–Sept; 16.00–00.00 Fri–Sun, Oct–Apr 🚌 Tram: Archivo de Indias; bus: C5

Beyond the centre

To the north, Santa Cruz merges into the large workaday district of
La Macarena, bordered to the west by the wide boulevard Alameda
de Hércules. There are several churches here, but the only real sight
is the basilica of La Macarena (see below), which stands next to
a surviving stretch of the city walls.

Head towards the river from Santa Cruz and the cathedral,
on the other hand, and you are immediately in El Arenal, the former
docksides. Here are two of the city's most distinctive monuments:
the bullring (see page 81) and the Torre del Oro (see page 82).
Follow the river and you will come to another interesting area of
sightseeing: the vast area of greenery which is the Parque de María
Luisa (see page 79). East from Santa Cruz, across Calle de Menéndez
y Pelayo, the sights vanish, but you might well be drawn to this
modern part of the city by its growing number of shops, bars
and nightspots.

SIGHTS & ATTRACTIONS

Basílica de la Macarena

Seville has always had a strong cult of the Virgin Mary. It has two
rival statues of the mother of Jesus which are ceremoniously brought
out during the Holy Week processions. One of them resides in Triana.
The other, possibly more famous, is housed here in this baroque
church built in 1949. The statue was carved in the late 17th century,
probably by the sculptress Luisa Roldán (or La Roldana), and its
expression is said to be something between a smile and sadness.
There's a museum dedicated to the Virgen de la Macarena and the
Brotherhood (*Hermandad*) which maintains her cult as well as a

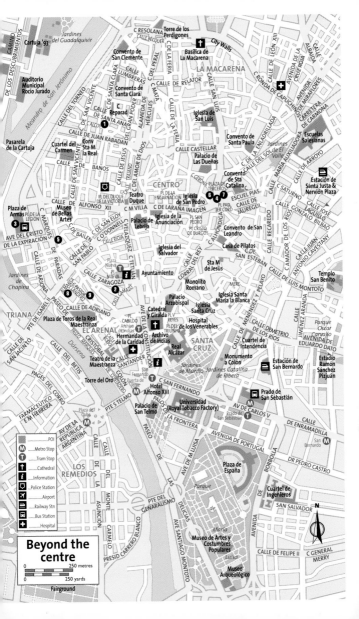

Beyond the
centre

| 0 | 250 metres |
| 0 | 250 yards |

Fairground

POI
Metro Stop
Tram Stop
Cathedral
Information
Police Station
Airport
Railway Stn
Bus Station
Hospital

shop selling devotional items. ⓐ C/ Bécquer 1 ⓣ (954) 90 18 00
ⓦ www.hermandaddelamacarena.es ⓛ 09.00–14.00, 17.00–21.00
Mon–Sat, 09.30–14.00, 17.00–21.00 Sun ⓝ Bus: 2, 10, 13, 14, C1–4

Hermandad de la Caridad

Still housing a hospice and community of nuns, this baroque former
almshouse was founded in the 17th century by Miguel de Mañara,
popularly believed to have been the inspiration for Don Juan. Legend
has it that he renounced his life of sin after a vision of his own death,
though versions vary. Whatever the case, as a former member of the
aristocracy he was able to use his contacts to secure some wonderful
paintings for the chapel, including six by his friend Bartolomé
Esteban Murillo and two stunning works by Juan de Valdés Leal.
ⓐ C/ Temprado 3, off C/ Santender ⓣ (954) 22 32 32 ⓦ www.santa-
caridad.org ⓛ 09.00–13.00 Mon–Fri, 09.00–12.30 Sat & Sun ⓝ Tram:
Archivo de Indias. Admission charge

Hotel Alfonso XIII

Seville's premier guesthouse is thought to be the only hotel ever
commissioned by a reigning monarch, having been built on the orders
of Alfonso XIII for heads of state visiting the 1929 Ibero-American
exhibition. He is lucky to have been immortalised in the name of
such a place, as in real life he was not so fortunate. His insensitive
meddling in political and military affairs forced him to abdicate in
1931 and go into exile. The hotel is in neo-Moorish style with a central
courtyard, sumptuous salons, grand corridors, an ornate lift, elegant
stained-glass panels, crystal chandeliers and many other exquisite
decorative touches. The best way to experience this place is to have a
drink in their charming patio bar. ⓐ C/ San Fernando 2 ⓣ (954) 91 70 00
ⓦ www.hotel-alfonsoxiii.es ⓝ Metro: Puerta de Jerez; tram: San Fernando

Parque de María Luisa & Plaza de España

In 1929 the city of Seville decided to transform a swathe of the grounds of the 17th-century Palacio de San Telmo into a fairground for the Ibero-American exhibition, a grand venture which bequeathed the city some extraordinary architecture as well as a superb park.

In particular, the Plaza de España is Seville at its extravagant, monumental best: a large semicircle of arcades ending in two mock baroque towers borrowed from the pilgrimage city of Santiago de Compostela in northern Spain. But what makes the Plaza de España shine, literally, are its ceramics. Following the curve of the building on the lowest level are technicoloured tiled benches representing the provinces of Spain in alphabetical order. The banisters of the bridges across its canal, meanwhile, are mini-masterpieces of the ceramicist's art. There are numerous entrances around the park's perimeter. ● 08.00–00.00 summer; 08.00–22.00 winter
Ⓜ Metro/tram: Prado de San Sebastián

🔺 *Exuberant ceramics at the Plaza de España*

Plaza de Toros de la Real Maestranza

Built in 1761, Seville's bullring is one of the oldest in Spain and certainly the most famous in the world. The bullring is owned by the Real Maestranza de Caballería (the Royal Corps of the Order of Chivalry of Seville), an organisation created around the time of the Reconquest to prepare and arm mounted knights for battle. It is a curious structure, not circular as might be expected but an irregular polygon made up of 30 sides of varying lengths with a white and ochre vernacular baroque façade looking onto the river bank. A capacity crowd is 13,934 spectators.

The arena itself is egg-shaped with the ground in it slightly higher in the centre than at the edges. Around the ring are all the facilities needed by the world of bullfighting: rooms for the *toreros* (toreadors) and their teams, a chapel (bullfighters are invariably deeply pious), infirmary, bull pens, a 'skinnery' (where dead bulls' hides are removed) and so on. The 20-minute guided visit takes in the highlights of the complex and the museum. This contains *trajes de luces* ('suits of lights' – the bullfighters' stunning outfits), paintings, bulls' heads and other bullfighting treasures.

The bullfighting season traditionally begins on Easter Sunday and ends in October. If you want to attend, there is a bewildering choice of seats. The cheapest are the top *gradas* in full sun (*sol*); the most expensive are those close to the ring in the shade (*sombra*). ⓐ Paseo de Cristóbal Colón 18 ❶ Museum: (954) 21 03 15; tickets: (954) 50 13 82 ⓦ www.realmaestranza.com ⏱ Museum: 09.30–20.00 May–Oct; 09.30–19.00 Nov–Apr; closes earlier on bullfight days ⓝ Tram: Archivo de Indias. Admission charge

---

◀ *The grand entrance of Spain's oldest bullring*

Torre del Oro

There's not much to this short, 12-sided tower on the banks of the River Guadalquivir north of the Puente de San Telmo, but it is still a well-known landmark. It was built in the 13th century by the Almohad rulers of southern Spain as part of their defences for the city. Why exactly it is called 'the Tower of Gold' is anyone's guess; at various times in its history it has served as wharf building, lighthouse, prison and chapel. Currently, it is a naval museum. ❸ Paseo de Cristóbal Colón ❶ (954) 22 24 19 ❺ 10.00–14.00 Tues–Fri, 11.00–14.00 Sat & Sun ❿ Metro: Puerta de Jerez; tram: San Fernando. Admission charge (free on Tues)

Torre de los Perdigones

Once part of an ammunitions factory, this 45 m (147 ft) tower was where the lead pellets (*perdigones*) were made. The factory was later turned into a park, but the tower has had a camera obscura added for a fascinating and unique view of Seville. ❸ C/ Resolana s/n ❶ 679 09 10 73 ❾ www.torredelosperdigones.com ❺ 10.00–13.30, 16.00–17.30 Tues–Sun; sessions every 30 mins ❿ Bus: 2, 10, 13, 14, C1–4. Admission charge

Universidad (Royal Tobacco Factory)

One of the most prized discoveries of the New World was tobacco and the majority of Europe's cigarettes were produced here in this vast, palatial factory building, which was completed in 1771 and now serves as part of Seville University. It can be hard to imagine the lives of the 3,000 female workers, *cigarreras*, who spent long working days rolling cigarettes on their thighs. Indeed, we probably wouldn't give them a second thought had they not inspired the world's most enduring musical (see page 86). ❸ C/ San Fernando ❶ (954) 55 10 00 ❾ www.us.es ❺ 09.00–21.00 Mon–Fri ❿ Tram: San Fernando

⬥ The 13th-century Torre del Oro stands on the banks of the Guadalquivir

THE CITY

CULTURE

Museo Arqueológico & Museo de Artes y Costumbres Populares (Archaeology Museum & Museum of Popular Arts & Customs)

At the far end of Parque de María Luisa, two museums face each other across Plaza de América, both of them occupying pavilions built for the 1929 exhibition. The more interesting is the Archaeological Museum, a neo-Renaissance building whose exhibits include the Treasure of the Carambolo – a collection of jewellery from the semi-mythical civilisation of Tartessos, which existed in Andalucia in the eighth and ninth centuries BC. The Museum of Popular Arts & Customs houses a collection of folk arts and crafts. ⓐ Pl. de América ⓘ Museo Arqueológico: (954) 23 24 01; Museo de Artes: (954) 23 25 76 ⓦ www.juntadeandalucia.es/cultura/museos/MASE ⓛ 14.30–20.30 Tues, 09.00–20.30 Wed–Sat, 09.00–14.30 Sun ⓒ Bus: 1, 6, 30, 31, 34, 36, 37. Admission charge (free for EU citizens)

Museo de Bellas Artes (Fine Arts Museum)

Seville's fine arts museum is claimed to be the second most important art gallery in Spain after the Prado in Madrid. It is housed in a 17th-century convent and has two floors arranged around three cloisters, all linked by a grand staircase. The building is appropriate since many of the works originally hung in convents and churches and are on religious themes. Although the museum has some sculpture and pieces of ceramics, jewellery and furniture (with exhibits dating from the Gothic period to the present day), the focus is on Seville's homegrown school of painting. The core of the collection is from three masters of Sevillian baroque: Zurbarán, Murillo and Valdés Leal. ⓐ Pl. del Museo 9, off C/ Alfonso XII ⓘ (954) 22 07 90 ⓦ www.juntadeandalucia.es/cultura/museos/MBASE

🔺 *The Museo de Bellas Artes houses one of Spain's most important art collections*

CARMEN

It's almost impossible to think of Seville's bullring without also thinking of Carmen, the tragic heroine of Bizet's opera of the same name. The story is based on an 1845 novella by Prosper Mérimée, who was inspired by a true story he heard from a countess while he was travelling in Spain. The eponymous Carmen is a strong-willed, mesmerising, manipulative young siren who attracts the attentions of a soldier, Don José, who is so besotted with her that he abandons his regiment. Carmen, however, spurns him in favour of a virile bullfighter, Escamillo. In a jealous rage, Don José springs on Carmen outside the bullring's Puerta del Príncipe and kills her as the crowds cheer Escamillo performing in the ring. The opera has proved to have an enduring appeal because it avoids easy moralising and Carmen, for all her faults, is likeable for her passion and her acceptance of her fate.

🕐 14.30–20.30 Tues, 09.00–20.30 Wed–Sat, 09.00–14.30 Sun
🚍 Bus: 6, 40, 43, C3–5. Admission charge (free for EU citizens)

RETAIL THERAPY

Antonio Bernal Get yourself a Spanish guitar made to order in this guitar builder's workshop across the road from Nervión Plaza. 🏠 C/ Herdando del Pulgar 20 📞 (954) 58 26 79
🌐 www.antoniobernal.com 🕐 10.00–14.00, 17.00–20.30 Mon–Fri, 10.00–14.00 Sat 🚇 Metro: Nervión

Farrutx Mallorcan designer Farrutx creates classic, sexy shoes for women (with a smaller line for men). 🅐 C/ Rioja 13 🅣 (954) 22 22 09 🅦 www.farrutx.com 🅛 10.00–13.30, 17.00–20.30 Mon–Fri, 10.00–12.00, 17.30–20.30 Sat 🅝 Bus: 13, 14, 40

Nervión Plaza Shopping centre between Santa Justa station and the football stadium. To get there on foot follow the remains of the Roman aqueduct along Calle Luis Montoto. 🅐 C/ de Luis Morales 3 🅣 (954) 98 91 31 🅦 www.nervionplaza.com 🅛 Shops: 10.00–22.00; restaurants: 10.00–03.00 (hours vary for individual establishments) 🅝 Metro: Nervión

Pedro Algaba Galdón A bullfighter's tailor: *trajes de luces* for hire or sale, but good ones don't come cheap. It takes a month and a team of 40 people to make a full suit. If you just want a souvenir, there are swords, capes, hats, sticks, banderillas, symbols, handkerchiefs, keyrings and posters. 🅐 C/ de Adriano 39 🅣 (954) 27 78 72 🅛 10.15–14.00, 17.15–20.30 Mon–Fri, 10.15–14.00 Sat 🅝 Tram: Archivo de Indias

Plaza de Armas A shopping and entertainment centre occupying the graceful engine shed of the former Córdoba railway station. 🅐 Pl. de la Legión 🅣 (954) 90 82 82 🅦 www.ccplazadearmas.com 🅛 10.00–22.00 (entertainment venues stay open later) 🅝 Bus: 6, 40, 43, B5, C3–5

Seville Football Club official shop If flamenco dresses, fans and shawls are not for you, you can always take home a sporting memento of Seville. 🅐 Estadio Ramón Sánchez Pizjuán, C/ Sevilla Fútbol Club 🅣 (954) 54 30 30 🅦 www.sevillafc.es 🅛 10.00–21.00 Mon–Sat 🅝 Metro: Nervión

Sombreros Padilla Crespo Handmade hats for all occasions: everything from top hats to Spanish equestrian hats. Hats are made to measure in your choice of fabric and colour and come with a guarantee. ⓐ C/ de Adriano 18B ⓣ (954) 56 44 14 ⓦ www.alaancha.com ⓛ 10.00–13.30, 17.00–20.30 Mon–Sat Ⓝ Tram: Archivo de Indias

TAKING A BREAK

Alcoy 10 £ ❶ A lively bar with tasty modern tapas that's a real gastronomic treat in this otherwise quiet residential part of town. ⓐ C/ Alcoy 10 ⓣ (954) 90 57 02 ⓛ 08.30–00.00 Tues–Sat, 08.30–16.00 Sun Ⓝ Bus: 13, 14

Bodeguita Antonio Romero £ ❷ The renowned selection of authentic Andalucian specialities available on the tapas menu – including a variety of *montaditos* (toasted sandwiches) – means that this place is often quite crowded. ⓐ C/ Gamazo 16 ⓣ (954) 21 05 85 ⓛ 12.00–01.00 Tues–Sun Ⓝ Tram: Plaza Nueva

La Fábrica £ ❸ No queues; no waiting: in this microbrewery bar you serve the beer yourself at a tap installed at your table. To go with the homebrew you can order tapas or a full meal. ⓐ Centro Comercial Plaza de Armas (see page 87) ⓣ (954) 90 88 28 ⓦ www.lafabrica-cerveceros.com ⓛ 12.00–01.00 Ⓝ Bus: 6, 40, 43, B5, C3–5

La Giganta £ ❹ What they call 'tapas' here are in fact full portions, so order conservatively. Try the wild mushrooms with Roquefort or beef with prunes. ⓐ C/ Alhóndiga 6 ⓣ (954) 21 09 75 ⓛ 12.00–16.30, 20.00–00.00 Tues–Sat, 12.00–16.30 Sun Ⓝ Bus: 32, C1, C2, C5

Las Piletas £ ❺ This early-opening café is a good option for breakfast. Tapas are available later in the day. ❸ C/ Marqués de Paradas 28 ❶ (954) 22 04 04 ❻ 07.30–00.00 ❼ Bus: 6, 40, 43, B5, C3–5

El Rinconcillo £ ❻ Seville's oldest bar is also one of its most atmospheric. ❸ C/ Gerona 40 ❶ (954) 22 31 83 ❼ www.elrinconcillo.es ❻ 13.00–01.00 ❼ Bus: 32, C1, C2

🔺 *Seville's tapas bars offer a wide variety of choice*

Taberna Manzanilla £ ➐ This small bar has tables spread in
the triangular square across the road from El Rinconcillo. It has a
good menu of tapas and also rents out rooms if you are in need of
somewhere to stay. **ⓐ** Pl. de Terceros 7 **❶** (954) 22 45 93 **🕑** 12.00–17.00,
20.00–00.00 (until 02.00 in summer) **Ⓝ** Bus: 32, C1, C2

AFTER DARK

RESTAURANTS
Asador Salas £ ➑ Meat, fish and shellfish grilled over a fire of
smouldering holm oakwood. **ⓐ** C/ Almansa 15 **❶** (954) 21 77 96
🕑 14.00–17.00, 20.00–01.00 **Ⓝ** Tram: Plaza Nueva

Porta Rossa £ ➒ An elegant but unpretentious Italian restaurant,
with superb fresh pasta dishes and a cosy ambience. **ⓐ** C/ Pastor
y Landero 20 **❶** (954) 21 61 39 **🕑** 14.00–15.45, 21.00–23.45 Tues–Sat,
14.00–15.45 Sun **Ⓝ** Tram: Plaza Nueva

LIVE MUSIC
El Ekeko A lively bar and cultural centre in La Macarena, run by
a Peruvian couple and offering anything from live music to art
exhibitions and literary events. **ⓐ** C/ Albaida 23 **❶** (954) 43 65 29
Ⓦ www.ekekobar.com **🕑** 20.00–00.30 (live music usually
Thur–Sat) **Ⓝ** Bus: 1

Sala FunClub Seville's longest-running club begins the night
with a concert and continues it as a bar. Eclectic agenda from
ethnic to electro. **ⓐ** Alameda de Hércules 86 **❶** 650 48 98 58
Ⓦ www.funclubsevilla.com **🕑** Concerts: 21.30; club: 00.00–07.00
Thur–Sat **Ⓝ** Bus: 13, 14

Terraza Capote A great place to be on a spring or summer evening. On Tuesdays you can enjoy flamenco with your cocktail and on Wednesdays it's theatre. Thursdays are given over to live Latin music. C/ Marqués de Contadero, next to Puente de Isabel II (954) 56 38 58 or 680 18 22 25 13.00–03.00 Apr–Oct Bus: 40, C4

FLAMENCO SHOWS

El Palacio Andaluz Dinner plus a flamenco show make for a fun but expensive night out. If you're counting your pennies swap dinner for a drink. C/ María Auxiliadora 1 (954) 53 47 20 www.elpalacioandaluz.com Shows: 21.30 (occasionally also 19.00) Bus: 1

Tablao El Arenal Having been in business since 1950, this is one of Seville's longest-running flamenco venues. C/ Rodo 7, between Arco del Postigo & Pl. de Toros (954) 21 64 92 www.tablaoelarenal.com Shows: 20.00 & 22.00 Tram: Archivo de Indias

CLUBS

Bauhaus Café Serves up electro-house, tech-house and nu-lounge. C/ Marqués de Paradas 53 (954) 22 42 10 12.00–03.00 Sun–Wed, 12.00–05.00 Thur–Sat Bus: 6, 40, 43, B5, C3–5

Buddha del Mar Chill out, funk, house, Latin, Spanish and international pop in the former railway station that is now the Plaza de Armas shopping centre. The restaurant serves Japanese, Thai and Chinese food. Centro Comercial Plaza de Armas (see page 87) (954) 08 90 95 15.30–03.00 Sun–Thur, 15.30–06.00 Fri & Sat Bus: 6, 40, 43, B5, C3–5. Admission charge Sat night

The river & beyond

Across the Guadalquivir from the city centre the city continues as a built-up island between two branches of the river. Step off the Puente de Isabel II, built of iron in 1852, and you'll find yourself in Triana, renowned as one of the cradles of flamenco and the source of all the beautiful ceramics to be seen in Seville. There are few sights as such but, if nothing else, you'll get some great views over the river.

To the south, Triana merges into the Barrio de los Remedios – nudging up to the site of the April Fair – which you will probably only stray into if you are looking for a particular shop, restaurant or club.

To the north, meanwhile, is the Isla de la Cartuja, an elongated strip of land rehabilitated for the Expo 92 world fair. Since that brief moment of glory, the Cartuja has been in search of a new vision to steer its future. Parts of the site have been 'repurposed' as an urban theme park and a technological business park, with offices and laboratories installed in some of expo's architecturally striking pavilions. But much of the Cartuja has a neglected feel with a disused cable car and Ariadne rocket now surrounded by fields of weeds – and not a shop, bar or restaurant in sight. In the middle of the Isla de la Cartuja stands an incongruous, schizophrenic monument: a monastery that was converted into a ceramics factory in the Industrial Revolution and now serves as a museum of contemporary art.

SIGHTS & ATTRACTIONS

Guadalquivir River & its bridges

The Guadalquivir River has formed the watery backbone of Seville since Roman times when merchant vessels sailed upstream to deposit one cargo and leave with another. Later, fleets rolled up laden with

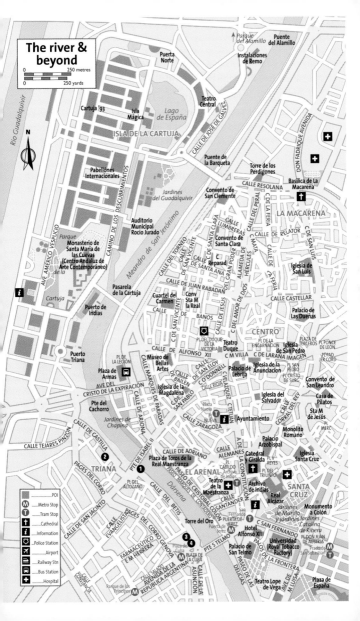

The river & beyond

0 — 250 metres
0 — 250 yards

Río Guadalquivir

N

Cartuja '93
Isla Mágica
Lago de España
ISLA DE LA CARTUJA
Teatro Central
Puerta Norte
Parque del Alamillo
Puente del Alamillo
Instalaciones de Remo

Pabellones Internacionales
Jardines del Guadalquivir
Puente de la Barqueta
Torre de los Perdigones
Basílica de la Macarena
LA MACARENA

Parque Américo Vespucio
Monasterio de Santa María de las Cuevas (Centro Andaluz de Arte Contemporáneo) de la Cartuja
Auditorio Municipal Rocío Jurado
Convento de San Clemente
CALLE RESOLANA
CALLE DE PERAL
CALLE DE LA FERIA
CALLE DE RELATOR
CALLE DE SAN LUIS
Iglesia de San Luis
CALLE DE LA FERIA

Pasarela de la Cartuja
Cuartel del Carmen
Conv Sta M la Real
CAMINO DE LOS DESCUBRIMIENTOS
Meandro de San Jerónimo
CALLE DEL TORNEO
CALLE DE SAN VICENTE
CALLE SANTA CLARA
Convento de Santa Clara
Reparad
CALLE DE SANTA ANA
ALAMEDA DE HERCULES
CALLE DEL GRAN PODER
CALLE DE JUAN RABADAN
CALLE DE AMOR DE DIOS
CALLE DE JESUS
BAÑOS
CALLE CASTELLAR
Palacio de Las Dueñas
CENTRO
PLAZA DE TERCEROS
PL PONCE DE LEON
Puerto de Indias
Puerto Triana
PL DE LA LEGIÓN
Museo de Bellas Artes
CALLE MARQUÉS DE PARADAS
CALLE DE BAILEN
CALLE DE ALFONSO XII
C M VILLA
CALLE DE SAN ELOY
CALLE DE O'DONNELL
CALLE RIOJA
PL DEL DUQUE DE LA VICTORIA
Teatro Duque
PL DE LA ENCARNACIÓN
CALLE DE LARAÑA
IMAGEN
Iglesia de San Pedro
PL SAN PEDRO
PL CRISTO DE BURGOS
Convento de San Leandro
Casa de Pilatos
Sta M de Jesús
PL MERC
Palacio de Lebrija
Iglesia de la Anunciación
Iglesia del Salvador
CORRAL DEL REY
Monolito Romano

Pte del Cachorro
Jardines de Chapina
AVE DEL CRISTO DE LA EXPIRACIÓN
CALLE DE ARJONA
Iglesia de la Magdalena
CALLE DE SAN PABLO
Plaza Nueva
CALLE ZARAGOZA
Ayuntamiento
Palacio Arzobispal
Iglesia Santa Cruz
SANTA CRUZ

CALLE DE CASTILLA
CALLE TEJARES PINZÓN
PTE DE ISABEL II
CALLE DE ADRIANO
Plaza de Toros de la Real Maestranza
Plaza de Toros de la Real Maestranza
EL ARENAL
Catedral Giralda
PL DEL CABILDO
Archivo de Indias
PLV REYES
PL DEL TRIUNFO
Real Alcázar
Monumento a Colón

TRIANA
PAGÉS DEL CORRO
PL DEL ALTOZANO
CALLE DE CRISTÓBAL
Teatro de la Maestranza
CALLE DE SAN FERNANDO
Jardines de Murillo y Jardines Catalina de Ribera
PAGÉS DEL CORRO
GENOVA
CALLE DEL BETIS
Dársena
CALLE ANTONIO
CALLE SANTANDER
Torre del Oro
PTE S TELMO
Puerta de Jerez
C SAN FERNANDO
Hotel Alfonso XIII
PUERTA DE JEREZ
Universidad (Royal Tobacco Factory)
PL DON JUAN DE AUSTRIA

CALLE EVANGELISTA
FARMACEUTICO E M HERRERA
Plaza de Cuba
PLAZA DE CUBA
Palacio de San Telmo
PALOS DE LA FRONTERA
San Sebastián
Fradique

CALLE SAN JACINTO
CALLE SALADO
AVENIDA DE REPÚBLICA ARGENTINA
AVENIDA DE LA ASUNCIÓN
Parque de los Príncipes
Teatro Lope de Vega
PASEO DE LAS DELICIAS
AVE DE M LUISA
Jardines de San Sebastián
Plaza de España

Legend:
- POI
- Ⓜ ...... Metro Stop
- Ⓣ ...... Tram Stop
- ✝ ...... Cathedral
- ⓘ ...... Information
- 🚓 ...... Police Station
- ✈ ...... Airport
- 🚉 ...... Railway Stn
- 🚌 ...... Bus Station
- ✚ ...... Hospital

gold and silver from the New World. There is still a functioning port, but it is largely dedicated to servicing tourist cruise ships.

The best bank to stroll along is on the city-centre side of the river, from the Torre del Oro to beyond the Plaza de Armas shopping centre. If you aren't feeling energetic, sit and enjoy the view from one of the bars and restaurants on Calle del Betis on the Triana side.

An even better way to enjoy the river is to take a short cruise with Cruceros Torre del Oro (see page 57).

The river is crossed by nine bridges, six of which were built for Expo 92. The two most interesting are the Puente del Alamillo (designed by the artist Santiago Calatrava) and the Puente de la Barqueta (opposite Isla Mágica theme park, see opposite), the most visible reminder of the heady days of the Expo for most Sevillanos.

🔺 Take a cruise boat and see the city from the river

Isla Mágica (Magic Island)

One of the few theme parks in the world in an urban area, the Magic Island is built around a lake on Isla de la Cartuja. It is loosely divided into eight zones and has over 40 rides, games, shows and other attractions – including a freefall tower, a 16th-century merry-go-round, various big dippers, a llama rodeo, rafting rivers and a '4 dimension' virtual reality experience. 🅐 C/ José de Gálvez, Isla de la Cartuja 🅘 Info: (902) 16 17 16; reservations: (902) 16 00 00 🅦 www.islamagica.es 🅛 Hours vary; often closed in low season so call to check 🅝 Bus: C1, C2

Triana

When you have drunk your fill of pretty-pretty Santa Cruz and seen enough of the grand monuments of central Seville, you might want to wander across the bridge into the more down-to-earth district of La Triana, which looks across the river at the bullring and the Torre del Oro. There are few historic sights here, but Triana has had plenty of history. To begin with it still bears its Roman name (deriving from Trajana, after the Emperor Trajan who was born in nearby Itálica). Later, less appealingly, Triana was an early home to the Spanish Inquisition as recalled by the name of one of its streets, Callejón de la Inquisición. Being a working-class, waterside neighbourhood, Triana has always been a rich recruiting ground for sailors and adventurers and supplied many shiphands bound for the Americas.

There are three good reasons for coming to modern Triana. First, even if you get no further than the end of the bridge, you will enjoy good views looking back at the city centre. Better still, take a seat at an outdoor table of one of the bars and restaurants along Calle del Betis, from which you can gaze at the Torre del Oro and the bullring

⬥ *Triana is the place to seek out authentic flamenco*

TRIANA CERAMICS

The first record of ceramics being produced in Triana dates from 1314, but it is widely accepted that the industry is much older than that. It is probable that the Romans produced amphorae here to transport oil and wine. In the Moorish period, Triana's potteries outside the city walls were busy producing the blue, white and green ceramic tiles, *azulejos*, that form such an essential part of interior decorations of buildings of the time. The characteristics of modern Triana pottery are considered to have been established by an Italian craftsman, Francisco Nicoloso Pisano, who settled in Triana at the end of the 15th century. In the 18th century, there was a great demand for painted tiles depicting religious images and realistic themes. Contemporary Triana ceramicists still make large mosaic scenes and signs for a variety of uses around the city.

and watch cruise ships come and go.

Second, this is the place to buy ceramics. It is the source of all the murals to be seen around central Seville and there are still about 40 functioning shops, studios, factories and workshops, most of which are open to visitors. The oldest and most popular is Cerámica Santa Ana (see page 100).

The third lure is flamenco. This is Seville's traditional gypsy quarter and proudly claims to be one of the birthplaces of flamenco (an honour tacitly shared with Jerez de la Frontera). Although you can see highly organised, professional shows in Santa Cruz, a purist would argue that you need to stumble on an impromptu combination of singer, guitarist and dancer swept up in the frenzy of spontaneous emotion

● *The colourful façade of Cerámica Santa Ana*

in some uncelebrated Triana dive to understand what flamenco is really about. Ⓝ Bus: 5, 6, 40, C1, C2

CULTURE

Monasterio de Santa María de las Cuevas (Centro Andaluz de Arte Contemporáneo)

In 1248, according to tradition, a statue of the Virgin Mary was found in one of the caves north of Triana from which clay to feed the potteries was extracted. A monastery dedicated to 'Our Lady of the Caves' grew up on the site. Columbus stayed in it, and his family had close links with it after his death. A magnificent ombu tree in its grounds is said to have been planted by Hernando Columbus, the son of the explorer.

The monastery was abandoned in 1835. Soon after, the buildings were leased by Charles Pickman, a merchant from Liverpool, who built kilns and installed machinery to churn out ceramics to meet local demand. Production continued into the 1970s.

In 1992 the monastery-factory formed a centrepiece for Seville's hosting of the world Expo. Since then it has housed Andalucia's contemporary art gallery, but this institution is rather cowed by its setting. At the heart of the complex is a rather plain church with a pretty Mudéjar patio off it in which the pallid statues of two nuns kneel at prayer.

But it's more the factory features that impress. A line of iron-girdered chimneys physically overshadow the other buildings, and there are various reminders that functional art was once churned

ELCANO'S ROUND-THE-WORLD VOYAGE

It's usually Magellan who is credited in the record books with the first circumnavigation of the globe, but this isn't quite accurate. Although he set off from Seville in command of a mission to sail around the world, he didn't make it back to claim the honour. Tragically, he was killed in a battle in the Philippines. So it was left to one his crewmen, a Spanish Basque, Juan Sebastián Elcano (whom Magellan had previously chained up and condemned to death for mutiny) to lead the expedition back to its starting point. On 8 September 1522 Elcano, along with the remaining 19 sailors from the 200 who had set out three years before, sailed into Seville on the only surviving ship of the expedition, the *Victoria*. Magellan may get all the mentions in history books, but at least Elcano has a street named after him in Triana.

out here to earn workers and masters a living. One entrance porch is entirely covered with neat rows of ornamental tiles like a salesman's samples book left permanently open. And the entrance on the river side of the monastery (not the main entrance) is a rather cute tiled gateway. ⓐ Av. Américo Vespucio 2 ① (955) 03 70 70 Ⓦ www.caac.es ① 10.00–20.00 Tues–Fri, 11.00–20.00 Sat, 11.00–15.00 Sun, Oct–Mar; 10.00–21.00 Tues–Fri, 11.00–21.00 Sat, 11.00–15.00 Sun, Apr–Sept Ⓝ Bus: C1, C2. Admission charge for gallery (free Tues for EU citizens)

RETAIL THERAPY

Cerámica Santa Ana Triana's most famous ceramics factory, which has been going since 1870. Reproduction historical pieces are available. ⓐ C/ San Jorge 31, off Pl. del Altozano ① (954) 33 39 90 ① 09.30–13.30, 16.30–22.00 winter; 09.30–13.30, 17.00–22.30 summer Ⓝ Bus: 5, 6, 40, C1, C2

Tierra Nuestra Seville's first specialist wine shop, and still arguably the best. ⓐ C/ Constancia 41 ① (954) 28 46 82 ① 17.00–22.30 Mon–Fri, 10.30–14.00 Sat Ⓝ Metro: Parque de los Príncipes

TAKING A BREAK

El Faro de Triana ££ ① The Triana Lighthouse ought to be classed as one of the city's landmarks, being a yellow tower with clock turret stuck to the end of Puente de Isabel II. Squeeze through the small bar and up the stairs where there are two small terraces with tables offering unbeatable views over the river. ⓐ Puente de Isabel II (Triana side) ① (954) 33 61 92 ① Restaurant: 11.00–16.30, 20.00–00.30; bar: 10.00–01.00 Ⓝ Bus: 5, 6, 40, C1, C2

🔺 *Puente de Isabel II with El Faro de Triana first on the left*

Sol y Sombra ££ ❷ One of the authentic old bars of Andalucia, decorated with bullfighting posters and serving tapas. ❸ C/ de Castilla 149–151 ❶ (954) 33 39 35 ⓦ www.tabernasolysombra.com ● 13.00–16.00, 20.30–00.00 ⓥ Bus: 5, 6, 40, C1, C2

AFTER DARK

RESTAURANTS

San Marco ££ ❸ Exquisite cuisine – Spanish with some Italian influence – in an elegant 18th-century house on the side of Calle del Betis away from the riverbank. ❸ C/ del Betis 68 ❶ (954) 28 03 10 ● 13.30–16.30, 20.30–00.30 Wed–Mon ⓥ Metro: Plaza de Cuba

Río Grande ££–£££ ❹ Three restaurants share terraces with more or less the same view. This one, strong on fish and seafood, is immediately next to Puente San Telmo. Next to it is the Asador de Triana and a little further on the Kiosco de las Flores. ⓐ C/ del Betis 31A ⓣ (954) 27 39 56 ⓦ www.riogrande-sevilla.com ⓛ 13.00–16.00, 20.00–00.00 ⓜ Metro: Plaza de Cuba

FLAMENCO SHOWS

Given its role in the history of flamenco, you would have thought Triana would be the best place to see the art form at its purest. And in one way that's true. The problem is tracking down authentic flamenco. All the most organised and well-advertised venues are back across the river in Santa Cruz and El Arenal. In Triana you have to keep your ears open and hope you stumble upon some bar where an impromptu performer has just acquired *el duende* – the indefinable spirit or passion that can't be bought or learned. Good places to start are **Casa Anselma** (ⓐ Pagés del Corro 49 ⓛ 20.00–02.00 Tues–Sun, July & Aug), very popular with locals for its spontaneous flamenco performances, and **Sala la Candelá** (ⓐ C/ Benito Mas & Prat 5 ⓣ 657 97 06 10 ⓛ 12.30–04.00 Tues–Sun). The clients here will be able to point you towards other hidden or up-and-coming venues in the area.

CLUBS

Discoteca Boss A discotheque on the banks of the Guadalquivir with a variety of levels and spaces at your disposal. ⓐ C/ del Betis 67 ⓣ (954) 99 01 04 ⓦ www.salaboss.es ⓛ 00.00–07.00 Wed–Sun ⓜ Metro: Plaza de Cuba

---

◗ *The lovely Andalucian 'white village' of Olvera*

OUT OF TOWN
trips

Days out from Seville

There are several places easily reached from Seville. Closest of them are the Roman ruins of Itálica (see page 108). Another rewarding short day trip is to the equally historic (but living) town of Carmona (see below). For fresh air and wildlife, meanwhile, you need to head straight for the outstanding Doñana National Park (see page 108). An hour to the south is the province of Cádiz and the city of Jerez de la Frontera (see page 110), famous for its sherries, dancing horses and flamenco music.

GETTING THERE

By rail
There are frequent trains between Jerez de la Frontera and Seville, leaving from the city's Santa Justa Station (see page 48).

By road
Lots of buses run every day to Carmona and Santiponce (in Itálica) from Plaza de Armas (see page 49). Ask for the schedule at the bus station and make sure you confirm the time of the last return bus. If you prefer to drive from Seville: for Itálica, take the A66 north to Santiponce; for Carmona, take the A4 northeast; for Doñana National Park, follow signs south from the west-bound A49; for Jerez de la Frontera, take the A4 or N4 south.

SIGHTS & ATTRACTIONS

Carmona
The historic town of Carmona, sitting on an outcrop of rock looking

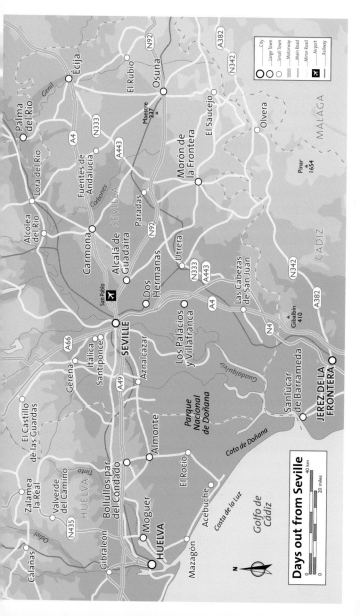

Days out from Seville

over plains, is an easy day trip or even half-day up the motorway from Seville. Both the Romans and the Moors have left an indelible mark on it. From the Moorish arch of the Puerta de Sevilla – which lets you through what's left of the ramparts – narrow streets climb up to the main square, the Plaza San Fernando, which is lined with some fine 17th- and 18th-century houses. The upper storeys of one corner house are photogenically faced in blue tiles.

Continue in the same direction and you'll come to the Gothic Iglesia de Santa María (on Plaza del Marqués de las Torres), which retains the ablutionary patio of the former mosque and also has a Visigothic calendar. Next to it is the **Museo de la Ciudad** (ⓐ Palacio Marqués de las Torres, San Ildefonso 1 ❶ (954) 14 01 28 ⓦ www.museociudad.carmona.org ❶ 11.00–14.00 Tues, 11.00–19.00 Wed–Mon. Admission charge) telling the story of Carmona from the Stone Age to the present day.

Further on, the town comes to an abrupt halt at another gateway, the Puerta de Córdoba, with its two octagonal towers. Beyond, the land drops steeply away. Retrace your steps and follow the signs to the parador, one of the state-run chain of hotels that often occupy historic buildings. This one is in the former fortress-palace of King Pedro I, which overhangs the cliff giving an unbroken view of the vast plain of sunflowers and cereals below where, in 206 BC, Scipio defeated Hasdrubal the Carthaginian in battle.

Outside the old town are two more Roman sites of interest: an amphitheatre (closed to the public, but you can see it from outside) and the Roman necropolis, the **Necrópolis Romana** (ⓐ Av. Jorge Bónsor 95 ❶ (955) 62 46 15 ⓦ www.juntadeandalucia.es/cultura/ museos/CAC ❶ 09.00–18.00 Tues–Fri, 09.00–13.30 Sat & Sun). Around 250 of the 800 family tombs that lie on the hillside in between the cypress trees have been excavated and put on display.

◐ *The Moorish Puerta de Sevilla at Carmona*

The largest have vestibules and one, the Servilia Tomb, is as big as a small villa. The so-called Elephant Tomb, meanwhile, has benches for funeral banquets and what's thought to have been a kitchen.

Tourist information 📍 Puerta de Sevilla ☎ (954) 19 09 55 🌐 www.turismo.carmona.org 🕐 10.00–18.00 Mon–Sat, 10.00–15.00 Sun

Itálica

Although Seville was founded by the Romans, it is long predated by its now insignificant neighbour, Itálica, at Santiponce just beyond the northern outskirts. This municipality was founded by Scipio Africanus

---

PARQUE NACIONAL DE DOÑANA (DOÑANA NATIONAL PARK)

The marshes, woods and sand dunes at the mouth of the Guadalquivir River make up one of Europe's largest and most important national parks.

Access is strictly controlled to protect the wildlife (most spectacularly the lynx and imperial eagle) that clings on in this fragile habitat, but Doñana's policy is one of controlling tourism rather than excluding it altogether.

There are five visitor centres on the fringes of the park, the one at Aznalcázar being the closest to Seville. Probably the best one to head for, though, is Acebuche, which can be reached via El Rocío (a town that is dead most of the year but springs to life for a big Whitsuntide pilgrimage – see Annual events, page 9).

All the visitor centres give out information and have displays about the flora and fauna in the park. But the only way to appreciate Doñana properly is to take a guided tour in a camouflaged bus. The trip takes four hours and covers 70 km (43 miles), taking in a representative sample of all the major ecosystems of the park. An alternative way to see a little of Doñana is to take a boat trip from the Fabrica de Hielo visitor centre at Bajo de Guía just outside Sanlúcar de Barrameda.

Of course, the wildlife you see depends on the time of year, the weather and luck. Most of the mammals in the park are difficult to spot and inevitably a lot of the interest is in the bird life. Doñana's marshes are on one of the main migration routes, and autumn and spring can be good times for birdwatching.

Aznalcázar Information Point ❶ (955) 75 02 09
Acebuche Visitor Centre ❶ (959) 43 04 32
Ⓦ www.donanavisitas.es
Guided tours ❸ Depart from Acebuche Visitor Centre ❺ 08.30 & 17.00 Mon–Sat, May–mid-Sept; 08.30 & 15.00 Tues–Sun, mid-Sept–Apr ❶ Booking essential
Boat trips ❸ Depart from Av. Bajo de Guía, Sanlúcar de Barrameda ❶ (956) 36 38 13 Ⓦ www.visitasdonana.com ❺ 09.00–20.00 Apr–Oct; 09.00–19.00 (tour times vary depending on season & numbers) ❶ Booking essential

in 206 BC to settle veteran soldiers of the Second Punic War. It was later the birthplace of the Emperor Trajan (born in AD 53), who ruled over the empire when it was at its maximum extent.

However, Itálica didn't reach the peak of its importance until the second century AD. Then, like the rest of the Roman Empire, it fell to the barbarian invasions of the fifth century. It was further ravaged in the eighth century by the Moors and its ruins subsequently

plundered for building materials, which were incorporated into the fabric of Seville. Its ruined streets and monuments are still impressive as ruins go – especially a round mosaic floor and the elliptical amphitheatre in which 25,000 spectators could cram to watch gladiatorial contests. The most interesting finds, though, are now in museums in Seville (and some of them in Madrid).

Information Centre ⓐ Av. de Extemadura 2, Santiponce ⓣ (955) 99 73 76 ⓦ www.juntadeandalucia.es/cultura/museos/CAI

Jerez de la Frontera

It may not sound like it, but this city gave its name to the world's most popular aperitif, sherry. In fact, *bodegas* producing fortified wines make up one half of Jerez's tourist appeal, and dancing horses make up the rest.

The **Fundación Real Escuela Andaluza de Arte Ecuestre** (Royal Horse School ⓐ Av. Duque de Abrantes ⓣ (956) 31 80 08 or 31 96 35 ⓦ www.realescuela.org ⓛ Opening & show times vary wildly – call or check website for exact date of intended visit. Admission charge) has got tourist management down to a fine art and if you like horses you shouldn't come away disappointed. You can take the full tour, which includes watching training sessions and visiting the stables, the tack room, the saddlery, the palace rooms, the Museum of Equestrian Arts and the Carriage Museum. Alternatively, if you are short of time or interest, you can opt for the slightly cheaper 'half visit'.

Better, though, is to see a show of the school's highly trained white steeds performing ballet routines. Best of all is to be here in May for Jerez's Feria del Caballo (Horse Fair) with its parades and dancing by both humans and animals. The soundtrack to this and other fiestas is flamenco music, of which Jerez claims to be one of the authentic cradles (along with Seville).

Jerez cathedral from a shady side street

● *Take a tour of the Bodega González Byass at Jerez*

As for sherry, you could fill a couple of days tasting and learning about it, but if you are just curious, visit one of the big *bodegas* such as **González Byass** (ⓐ C/ Manuel María González 12 ❶ (956) 35 70 16 Ⓦ www.bodegastiopepe.com ● Tours: 11.30, 12.30, 13.30, 15.30, 16.30 & 17.30 Sept–June; 11.30, 12.30, 13.30, 16.30, 17.30 & 18.30 Jul & Aug) – home of Tío Pepe, supposedly Spain's best-known brand abroad – or **Domecq** (ⓐ C/ San Ildefonso 3 ❶ (956) 15 15 00 Ⓦ www.domecqbodegas.com ● Tours: 10.00, 11.00, 12.00, 13.00, other times by appointment). **Tourist information** ⓐ Edificio los Claustros, Alameda Cristina ❶ (956) 34 17 11 or 33 88 74 Ⓦ www.turismojerez.com

RETAIL THERAPY

La Casa del Jerez Sells souvenirs of Jerez and gives you the opportunity

to taste wines before you buy. ⓐ Urbanización Divina Pastora Local 3
(opposite the Real Escuela Andaluza del Arte Ecuestre) ⓣ (956) 33 51 84
ⓛ 10.00–15.00, 18.00–21.00 Mon–Fri, 10.00–15.00 Sat

TAKING A BREAK

Carmona
Mesón Sierra Mayor £–££ This atmospheric bar-restaurant occupies
the old stables of the historic mansion which contains Carmona's
museum (see page 106). It specialises in *jamón ibérico* (cured ham);
the best quality is known as *pata negra*. ⓐ C/ San Ildefonso 1 (inside
Museo de la Ciudad, see page 106) ⓣ (954) 14 44 04 ⓛ 12.00–23.00
Mon–Sat

Restaurante Tabanco ££ Located inside the Alcázar de la Reina hotel,
this restaurant has a lovely shaded patio which is great for long,
lazy lunches in summer. ⓐ C/ Hermana Concepción Orellana 2
ⓣ (954) 19 62 00 ⓦ www.alcazar-reina.es ⓛ 13.00–16.30, 20.30–23.30

La Yedra ££ A restaurant in a pleasing courtyard near the parador.
ⓐ C/ General Freire 8 ⓣ (954) 14 45 25 ⓦ www.restaurantelayedra.es
ⓛ 13.00–16.15, 20.30–23.15 Tues–Sat, 13.00–16.15 Sun

Jerez de la Frontera
El Gallo Azul £ A semicircular bar with dining room above commanding
a view of the street life of Jerez, such as it is (it vanishes when the
shops close). ⓐ C/ Larga 2 ⓣ (956) 32 61 48 ⓛ 11.30–00.00 Mon–Sat

Juanito ££ An old bar famous for serving the best tapas in town.
ⓐ C/ Pescadería Vieja 8–10 ⓣ (956) 33 48 38 ⓛ 13.00–17.00, 20.30–23.00

Sanlúcar de Barrameda

Mirador de Doñana ££ One of a number of waterside restaurants with a view across the beach and river to the national park. Fish and seafood on the menu. ⓐ Bajo de Guia, Sanlúcar de Barrameda ⓘ (956) 36 42 05 ⓛ 13.15–16.30, 20.15–00.00 Mon–Sat

AFTER DARK

Jerez de la Frontera

La Taberna Flamenca £ A flamenco restaurant housed in a former *bodega*. ⓐ Angostillo de Santiago 3, in front of Iglesia de Santiago ⓘ (956) 32 36 93 ⓦ www.latabernaflamenca.com ⓛ 13.30–16.00, 20.00–00.00 June–Oct; 12.00–16.00, 20.00–00.00 Tues–Sat; show times vary (call to check and reserve)

ACCOMMODATION

Carmona

El Rincón de las Descalzas ££ A small, homely hotel around three flowery patios in which the peace is only disturbed by the sound of classical music and a trickling fountain. ⓐ C/ Descalzas 1 ⓘ (954) 19 11 72 ⓦ www.elrincondelasdescalzas.com

Casa de Carmona £££ A luxurious hotel that unashamedly offers a taste of 'the lifestyle of the authentic Spanish nobility'. ⓐ Pl. de Lasso 1 ⓘ (954) 19 10 00 ⓦ www.casadecarmona.com

Parador de Carmona £££ The principal monument of Carmona, its 14th-century castle, is also its finest hotel with a tremendous view over the plains. At the foot of the cliff is the parador's enticing

swimming pool. ⓐ Alcázar del Rey Don Pedro ⓣ (954) 14 10 10
ⓦ www.parador.es

Jerez de la Frontera
Bellas Artes ££ An old stone house restored using authentic
materials. Individually styled rooms. Private car park for guests.
ⓐ Pl. del Arroyo 45 ⓣ (956) 34 84 30 ⓦ www.hotelbellasartes.com

Palacio Garvey ££–£££ Restored 1850 neoclassical mansion in the
old part of Jerez. Small swimming pool. No time limit for breakfast.
Access for guests with disabilities. ⓐ Pl. Rafael Rivero, Tornería 24
ⓣ (956) 32 67 00 ⓦ www.sferahoteles.com

Casa Viña de Alcántara £££ A luxury boutique hotel with extensive
grounds, a swimming pool in the garden and an almost colonial
feel. Only nine rooms so book early. ⓐ Carretera Jerez–Arcos de la
Frontera (A382) ⓣ (956) 39 30 10 ⓦ www.vinadealcantara.com

El Rocío
Hotel La Malvasia ££ An unexpected find in sleepy, remote El Rocío,
this is a sumptuously designed boutique hotel, with a great restaurant,
for very reasonable rates. ⓐ C/ Sanlúcar 38 ⓣ (959) 44 38 70
ⓦ www.lamalvasiahotel.com

Sanlúcar de Barrameda
Los Helechos £ A friendly, bright, white, plant-filled hotel, close to
the departure point for the Doñana boat excursions (see page 109).
The hotel's pleasant café is open from 08.00–00.00 every day. ⓐ Pl.
Madre de Dios 9 ⓣ (956) 36 76 55 ⓦ www.hotelloshelechos.com

The white villages & towns

Brilliantly whitewashed hill towns and villages, often occupying dramatic sites and laid out higgledy-piggledy across the contours, are emblematic of Andalucia. The most picturesque of *los pueblos blancos* are concentrated in the sierras of Cádiz province, southeast of Seville, within the range of an overnight trip from the city. Several of these towns are still looked down upon by indomitable medieval fortresses, and their narrow, shady streets have changed little over the centuries. The countryside is often ruggedly spectacular, and the mountains make excellent territory for hiking, biking and nature-watching.

GETTING THERE

By road
You'll need a car to explore properly. Take the N4 or A4 south towards Jerez de la Frontera, then turn off left to Arcos de la Frontera. From here, the A372 branches off for El Bosque and Grazalema. A scenic road climbs over the pass between Grazalema and Zahara de la Sierra. From there you can work your way southeast to Ronda. If you don't have a car, there are daily buses to Ronda from the Plaza de Armas bus station in Seville.

SIGHTS & ATTRACTIONS

Arcos de la Frontera
The point of access to The white villages and towns from Seville is Arcos de la Frontera, which, despite the expanding modern estates of houses around its fringes, has an unchanging old heart at the

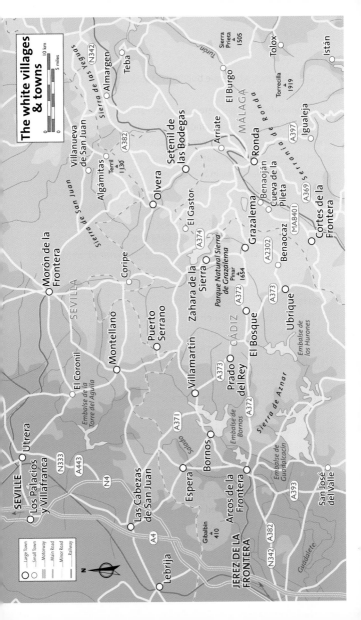

The white villages & towns

◯	Large Town
○	Small Town
	Motorway
	Main Road
	Minor Road
	Railway

0 5 miles
0 10 km

SEVILLE
Utrera
Los Palacios y Villafranca
N333
A443
N4
Lebrija
A4
Las Cabezas de San Juan
Espera
Bornos
Gibalbín 410
JEREZ DE LA FRONTERA
N342 A382
Arcos de la Frontera
A393
San José del Valle
Guadalete
Embalse de Guadalcacín
A371
El Coronil
SEVILLA
Morón de la Frontera
Montellano
Puerto Serrano
Coripe
Villamartín
A373
Prado del Rey
A372
CÁDIZ
Embalse de Bornos
Sierra de Aznar
Embalse de la Torre del Aguila
Salado
Embalse de los Hurones
Ubrique
El Bosque
A373
A372
Zahara de la Sierra
Parque Natural Sierra de Grazalema
Pinar 1654
A374
El Gastor
Olvera
Algámitas
Terril 1130
Villanueva de San Juan
Sierra de san juan
Sierra de los yeguas
Almargen
Teba
N342
Setenil de las Bodegas
Arriate
Ronda
MÁLAGA
Benaoján
Cueva de la Pileta
MA8401
A2302
Benaocaz
Grazalema
Cortes de la Frontera
A369
A397
Igualeja
Serranía de Ronda
El Burgo
Sierra Prieta 1505
Tolox
Istán
Torrecilla 1919
Turón
N

top of the town where the buildings creep right up to the lip of a breathtaking precipice.

The best way to get here is to drive. Park in the Plaza de España if you are travelling by car and walk up Calle Corredera to the main square of the old part of town, the Plaza del Cabildo. This is overlooked by the church of Santa María de la Asunción, whose west façade takes on a golden glow in the afternoon sun. To one side of the square a balcony provides views over the countryside below. Most of Arcos' shops, bars, hotels and restaurants are in the narrow streets around the Plaza del Cabildo.

Tourist information ⓐ Pl. del Cabildo ⓣ (956) 70 22 64 ⓦ www.arcosdelafrontera.es ⓛ 10.00–14.30, 16.00–19.00 Mon–Fri, 10.30–13.30, 16.00–18.00 Sat, 10.30–13.30 Sun

Grazalema

It may well be raining when you visit Grazalema because this is the place with the highest rainfall in Spain (by quantity of water falling, not number of wet days). That said, at least it keeps the surrounding countryside green.

Overlooked by crags of limestone, the town is used as a base by visitors to the nearby nature reserve of the same name, which is good for birdwatching, botanising or just walking around. The town itself has a small traditional weaving industry making blankets (see page 124).

From Grazalema (best reached by car), a scenic road climbs over the Puerto de las Palomas (Doves' Pass), through a natural park. You go through forests that harbour a rare species of tree, the Spanish fir (*Abies pinsapo*). The tree grows in only a few areas of Spain and Morocco and is a protected species. Above the cliffs you are likely to see vultures soaring overhead.

Tourist information ⓐ Pl. de España 11 ⓣ (956) 13 20 73 ⓛ 10.00–14.00,

● *The beautiful old buildings in Arcos de la Frontera*

CUEVA DE LA PILETA

This extensive cave contains some of the best and most curious prehistoric art in Europe: symbols in yellow and red; 360 feathery characters that may be some kind of writing (although the language may never be deciphered); and representations of animals, including a large fish. The paintings here were created at the same time as, or perhaps even earlier than, the more famous ones at Altamira in northern Spain. However, their significance, as with all prehistoric art, remains a matter of conjecture.

Interestingly, the cave was only found in 1905, by a local farmer who was hunting for bat droppings; it was not until six years later that a British ornithologist, Colonel Willoughby Verner, identified it as prehistoric.

Visits are by guided tour only, lasting around an hour. Numbers are limited, but it is possible to reserve a place by phone only on the first tour of the day. ⓐ 4 km (2½ miles) from Benaoján off the MA8401 towards Cortes de la Frontera ⓘ (952) 16 73 43 ⓦ www.cuevadelapileta.org ⓛ Tours: 10.00–13.00, 16.00–17.00 (until 18.00 in summer). Admission charge

16.00–20.00 Mon–Fri, 10.00–20.00 Sat & Sun, Nov–Apr; 10.00–14.00, 16.00–21.00 Mon–Fri, 10.00–21.00 Sat & Sun, May–Oct

Ronda

It's hard to imagine a more dramatic site for a town than on the edge of a cliff and astride a gorge. Ronda is justly the most famous of the white villages and towns and also the most touristy because of its

🔺 *A typical* cortijo, or farmhouse, near Arcos de la Frontera

proximity to the Costa del Sol.

The town is literally cut in two by a 90 m (295 ft) deep gorge (El Tajo) of the River Guadalevín. Puente Nuevo (New Bridge), a feat of 18th-century engineering, crosses it. Its central section was once used as a prison. To get the best view of it, take the path down into the gorge from Plaza del Campillo (at the end of Calle Tenorio) or drive down Camino de los Molinos (from the Almocabar Gate) and climb up to the Arabic Arch. A visitor centre explains the history of the bridge with an audiovisual presentation.

The next most popular sight in Ronda is the bullring, the **Plaza de Toros** (🅐 C/ Virgen de la Paz 15 ☎ (952) 87 41 32 🕐 10.00–18.00 Nov–Feb; 10.00–19.00 Mar; 10.00–20.00 Apr–Oct), which is the oldest in Spain and contains a bullfighting museum. The standard, modern form of bullfighting – on foot rather than on horseback –

🔺 *The incredible El Tajo gorge at Ronda*

originated in Ronda in the 18th century, and this is commemorated by a 'Goya-esque' bullfight in period dress in September. Ronda has produced two famous 'dynasties' of bullfighters, the Romeros and the Ordóñezs. Arguably the most successful bullfighter ever was Pedro Romero, who retired in 1799 remarking: 'Bearing in mind the 28 years that I have been killing bulls, on average 200 bulls a year, I reckon that I have killed approximately 5,600 bulls, if not more.' And all without suffering a single scratch. Attached to the bullring is a museum of bullfighting, the **Museo Taurino** (ⓐ C/ Virgen de la Paz 15 ⓣ (952) 87 41 32 ⓛ 10.00–18.00 Nov–Feb; 10.00–19.00 Mar; 10.00–20.00 Apr–Oct).

The town has half a dozen other museums, of which the most interesting is the **Museo del Bandolero** (ⓐ C/ Armiñan 65 ⓣ (952) 87 77 85 ⓦ www.museobandolero.com ⓛ 10.30–20.00 summer; 10.30–19.00 winter), whose theme is banditry in the surrounding mountains.

One other essential sight is the best-preserved suite of Moorish baths (Baños Árabes) in Spain, which have brick horseshoe arches holding up barrel vaults pierced with star-shaped skylights.

Tourist information ⓐ Paseo de Blas Infante ⓣ (952) 18 71 19 ⓦ www.turismoderonda.es ⓛ 10.00–19.00 Mon–Fri (until 18.00 in winter), 10.00–14.00, 15.00–17.00 Sat, 10.00–14.30 Sun

Setenil de las Bodegas

Setenil is an atypical white town because of its site. Rather than being high up on a crag or hillside it winds through a gorge, using the rock overhangs as roofs for some of its houses and transforming one street into a tunnel. In the middle of it is a 16th-century church on a rock next to an Arab tower, from the battlements of which you can get a view of the town.

Tourist information ⓐ C/ Villa 2 ⓣ (956) 13 42 61 or 659 54 66 26 ⓦ www.setenil.com ⓛ 10.30–14.00, 16.00–19.00 Tues–Sun

Zahara de la Sierra

A compact zigzag cluster of white houses at the base of a rock crowned by a castle, Zahara has a strong claim to be the prettiest of the white villages and towns. There are not many streets, but they are pleasant to stroll around. Naturally, there are great views from

the castle if you can face a stiff 10–15-minute walk. At Corpus Christi (May or June) the streets of Zahara are decorated with an impressive mass of greenery brought in from the surrounding countryside.

RETAIL THERAPY

Artesanía Textil de Grazalema Maintains the traditional woollen industry. Its small factory, in which blankets and ponchos are woven from local wool using hand-operated looms, is open to the public. Products are on sale in a shop on the premises. ❸ Carretera de Ronda, Grazalema ❶ (956) 13 20 08 ❿ www.mantasdegrazalema.com ❺ 08.00–14.00, 15.00–18.30 Mon–Thur, 08.00–14.00 Fri

TAKING A BREAK

Arcos de la Frontera
Marqués de Torresoto £ The restaurant inside the Marqués de Torresoto hotel (see page 126) is in the shady central courtyard, a useful stop for lunch or dinner. ❸ C/ Marqués de Torresoto 4 ❶ (956) 70 07 17 ❿ www.hotelmarquesdetorresoto.com ❺ 13.00–16.00, 20.00–23.30 Wed–Mon

Mesón el Patio £ An efficient, family-run restaurant in the old part of town serving traditional homemade food. There's a choice of four set menus all at the same very reasonable price. There's also a *pensión* in which some of the rooms have terraces with views. ❸ Callejón de las Monjas 4 ❶ (956) 70 23 02 ❿ www.mesonelpatio.com ❺ 12.00–17.00, 19.30–23.00 Thur–Tues

Parador de Arcos de la Frontera ££–£££ The restaurant inside the lovely

Parador (see page 126) has magnificent views over the old town and rolling countryside. Expect high quality cuisine at high prices and do try the 12-course tasting menu – it's worth it. ⓐ Pl. del Cabildo ❶ (956) 70 05 00 Ⓦ www.parador.es ❶ 10.30–23.00

Ronda

Faustino £ An energetic couple run this old-fashioned bar, cluttered with bullfighting and flamenco memorabilia. Food is no-frills and it's good value for what you get. ⓐ C/ Santa Cecilia 4 ❶ (952) 19 03 07 ❶ Tues–Sun (exact times vary)

Almocábar ££ In the residential Barrio de San Francisco at the south end of town is this superb tapas bar and restaurant, where the speciality is beef served sizzling on a tablet of hot volcanic stone. ⓐ Pl. Ruedo Alameda 5 ❶ (952) 87 59 77 ❶ 12.30–16.30, 20.00–00.00

Tragatapas ££ Baby sister of Tragabuches (see below), this innovative tapas restaurant also boats an impressive wine list. Popular with Ronda's younger residents. ⓐ C/ Nueva 4 ❶ (952) 87 72 09 ❶ 12.00–16.30, 20.00–00.00 Tues–Sat, 12.00–16.30 Sun

Tragabuches ££–£££ Creative gastronomy is served up at this top-class restaurant. Book early. ⓐ C/ José Aparicio 1 ❶ (952) 19 02 91 Ⓦ www.tragabuches.com ❶ 13.30–15.30, 20.30–22.30 Tues–Sat, 13.30–15.30 Sun

Setenil de las Bodegas

Las Flores £ A village bar-restaurant serving straightforward but wholesome food. ⓐ Av. del Carmen 24 ❶ (956) 12 40 44 ❶ 10.00–23.00

ACCOMMODATION

Arcos de la Frontera

La Casa Grande £–££ Boutique hotel in the old part of town with a rooftop terrace for relaxing. ⓐ C/ Maldonado 10 ⓣ (956) 70 39 30 ⓦ www.lacasagrande.net

Marqués de Torresoto £–££ A comfortable 17th-century aristocratic house in the old part of town next to the church and the main square. Restaurant on the patio. ⓐ C/ Marqués de Torresoto 4 ⓣ (956) 70 07 17 ⓦ www.hotelmarquesdetorresoto.com

Parador de Arcos de la Frontera ££–£££ Part of the renowned Parador hotel group, this beautiful old house on the banks of the Guadalete river is the best place to stay in town. ⓐ Pl. del Cabildo ⓣ (956) 70 05 00 ⓦ www.parador.es

Grazalema

La Casa de las Piedras £ A converted house in one of the oldest streets in the town. The bedrooms, around a patio, are simply but charmingly furnished and the beds spread with locally made Grazalema blankets. ⓐ C/ de las Piedras 32 ⓣ (956) 13 20 14 ⓦ www.casadelaspiedras.net

Ronda

Arriadh £ A five-room hotel with views near Arriate, just outside Ronda. ⓐ Camino de Laura ⓣ (952) 11 43 70 ⓦ www.arriadhhotel.com

Jardín de la Muralla ££ An elegant country-house hotel to the south of town, with far-reaching views from its garden and pool area, and a cosy lounge filled with books. ❸ C/ Espíritu Santo 13 ❶ (952) 87 27 64 ❿ www.jardindelamuralla.com

Molino del Arco ££ Family-run guesthouse in a converted olive oil mill. ❸ C/ Partido de los Frontones, 8 km (5 miles) from Ronda ❶ (952) 11 40 17 ❿ www.hotelmolinodelarco.com

Molino del Santo ££ Once a watermill, now a sun-trap with a pleasing swimming pool. 12 km (just over 7 miles) from Ronda. ❸ Barrada de la Estación, Benaoján ❶ (952) 16 71 51 ❿ www.molinodelsanto.com

Zahara de la Sierra
Marqués de Zahara £ Large old house around a central patio converted into an 11-room hotel and restaurant. ❸ C/ San Juan 3 ❶ (956) 12 30 61 ❿ www.marquesdezahara.com

🔺 *Horses graze in an olive grove near Ronda*

Córdoba, Granada & the surrounding towns

Seville is one of the three great cities of Andalucia associated with the medieval Muslim civilisation of Spain. It would be a shame to leave without seeing the other two, Córdoba and Granada. They are easily reached by motorway and have one world-famous monument apiece plus a host of other sights worth visiting. All three cities have very different atmospheres and are, incidentally, packed with bars and restaurants.

Dotted around them are several charming towns that complement the cities – and each other – perfectly.

GETTING THERE

By road

Córdoba is to the northeast of Seville, reachable by road on the A4. There is just one drawback to driving to Córdoba: parking. The best policy is to head straight for the nearby underground multi-storey car park (Av. del Aeropuerto – which, as its name suggests, goes towards the airport).

Granada is to the east of Seville, most easily reached by road by taking the A4 to Córdoba, then the N432. The town of Écija is just off the A4 motorway. To drive to Antequera from Seville, take the A4 and N331, and for Osuna, take the A92.

CÓRDOBA

Roman Córdoba was the capital of southern Spain, but it was after the Muslim invasion of Spain in the eighth century that it truly came into its own. In the tenth and eleventh centuries, while the

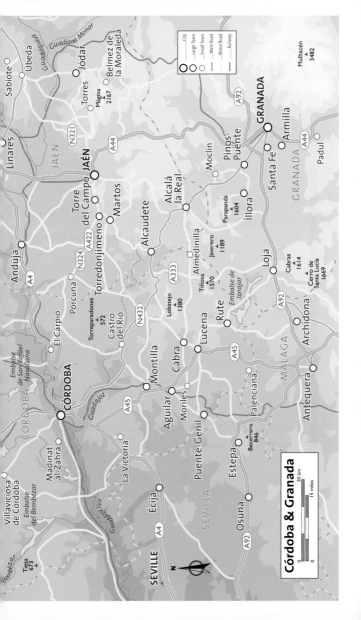

Córdoba & Granada

rest of Europe was wallowing in the dark ages, the civilised place to be was in Muslim Córdoba where Christians and Jews added to a cultural melting pot, and art and learning thrived.

Tourist information 🅐 C/ Rey Heredia 22 🅣 (957) 20 17 74
🅦 www.turismodecordoba.org

MADINAT AL-ZAHRA

When Muslim Córdoba was at the height of its wealth and power in the 10th century, caliph Abd al-Rahman III decided to build himself a new administrative city-cum-royal residence at the foot of the Sierra Morena that would put medieval Christian Europe to shame. One chronicler speaks of 10,000 men working daily on the vast building site, yet Madinat al-Zahra was to last only 70 years before being sacked in a civil war.

Madinat is the third biggest archaeological dig in Europe after Pompeii and Crete, but only a tenth of its ruins have so far been uncovered. What you see today is a mixture of original remains and reconstruction using modern materials to imitate the originals.

The most interesting part is the Salon de Abd al-Rahman, the only roofed building (towards the bottom of the site), which has arcades of gracious horseshoe arches and rich decoration on its walls and the capitals of columns. 🅐 Madinat is just under 10 km (6 miles) west of Córdoba off the main road towards Palma del Río, well signposted from the city centre 🅣 (957) 32 91 30 🅦 www.juntadeandalucia.es/cultura/museos/CAMA 🅛 10.00–18.30 Tues–Sat, 10.00–14.00 Sun, mid-Sept–Apr; 10.00–20.30 Tues–Sat, 10.00–14.00 Sun, May–mid-Sept

CÓRDOBA, GRANADA & THE SURROUNDING TOWNS

SIGHTS & ATTRACTIONS

La Mezquita-Catedral

Much of Córdoba's immense attraction derives from its historical religious significance. The magnificence that once typified the city can be seen in the famous *mezquita*, or mosque, that dominates the city centre. Built on the site of a Visigothic church, it is the work

⬥ *The Moorish palace at Madinat al-Zahra*

131

of four caliphs. What impresses is the immense size of the Hall of Caliph Abd al-Rahman. It is the only building on the site that has a roof, which is supported by over 800 two-tier horseshoe arches rising from slender columns (many of which are recycled from Roman and Visigothic buildings). Because the whole area slopes downhill, you enter from above, and the Hall is near the bottom. On the southern wall is a *mihrab* – prayer niche decorated with intricate plasterwork and mosaics.

When Córdoba was reconquered by the Christians they couldn't leave such a structure untouched to testify to the success of their rival religion. Thus, in the 16th century a cathedral was dropped

🔺 *A Moorish patio in Córdoba*

incongruously into the middle of the Hall. The old minaret was simultaneously dressed up as a belfry.

Take a walk around the Judería, the old Jewish quarter of the city near the mosque. This is a delightful jumble of shady alleyways and whitewashed houses decorated with wrought iron grilles and flowerpots. Look out for the *Sinagoga*, synagogue (🕾 (957) 20 29 28), no more than a delightful square hall with richly decorated walls, and one of the only three remaining in Spain. 🅐 C/ Torrijos 🕾 (957) 47 05 12 🕘 08.30–18.00 Mon–Sat, 08.30–10.00, 14.00–18.00 Sun; mass: 11.00 Sun (times may vary). Admission charge (free before 10.00 Mon–Sat)

RETAIL THERAPY
Zoco Municipal de Artesanía A pretty courtyard close to the synagogue that's occupied by craftsmen and women who can be seen at work in their studios. There's a shop selling their wares as you come in off the street. 🅐 C/ Judíos 🕾 (957) 29 05 75 🅦 www.artesaniadecordoba.com 🕘 10.00–20.00 Mar–Nov; 10.00–19.00 Mon–Fri, 11.00–14.00 Sat & Sun, Dec–Feb

TAKING A BREAK
Córdoba's usually sunny weather and beautiful streets, buildings and parks make it ideal for picnicking. Buy a *bocadillo* (sandwich) from a café and soak up the atmosphere.

Taberna San Miguel £ Better known as 'El Pisto', a well-known old bar on a bullfighting theme where tapas are served along with Montilla-Moriles wines (the local equivalent of sherry). 🅐 Pl. San Miguel 1 🕾 (957) 47 01 66 🅦 www.casaelpisto.com 🕘 12.00–16.00, 20.00–00.00 Mon–Sat, 12.00–16.00 Sun

AFTER DARK
Restaurants
Casa Pepe de la Judería ££ Tapas downstairs around the patio; restaurant upstairs. ⓐ C/ Romero 1 ⓣ (957) 20 07 44 ⓦ www.cabezasromero.com ⓛ 13.00–16.00, 20.30–23.30

Bodegas Campos £££ Wine *bodega* transformed into a restaurant. A delightful place in itself, with excellent food. ⓐ C/ Almireceros 1–3 (corner C/ Elvira) ⓣ (957) 49 75 00 ⓦ www.bodegascampos.com ⓛ 13.00–17.00, 20.30–00.00 Mon–Sat, 13.00–17.00 Sun

El Churrasco £££ The city's classic restaurant is dispersed around several patios and other pleasant dining spaces. Specialises in grilled meats. ⓐ C/ Romero 16 ⓣ (957) 29 08 19 ⓦ www.elchurrasco.com ⓛ 13.00–16.00, 20.30–00.00

Flamenco shows
El Cardenal This venue puts on a flamenco show six nights a week. ⓐ C/ Torrijos 10 ⓣ (957) 48 32 21 ⓦ www.tablaocardenal.com ⓛ Mon–Sat (hours vary)

ACCOMMODATION
Casa de los Naranjos ££ A small hotel with just 20 rooms in the old part of the city. Some of the furnishings were made by local craftsworkers. Internet access available. ⓐ C/ Isabel Losa 8 ⓣ (957) 47 05 87 ⓦ www.casadelosnaranjos.com

Lola ££–£££ Any hotel that dares to advertise itself as 'the most beautiful hotel in Andalucia' must be worth taking a chance on. Each of the eight rooms is individually furnished with a touch of

homeliness. Close to the mosque. ❷ C/ Romero 3 ❶ (957) 20 03 05
🌐 www.hotelconencantolola.com

GRANADA

After a stint as the Roman city of Illibris, Granada passed into
Jewish hands before being taken over by Moors. The result is
a culturally fascinating city, which, incidentally, is now famous
for its buzzing nightlife.

SIGHTS & ATTRACTIONS
La Alhambra
As the last Muslim city of Spain to fall to the Christian reconquest
(in 1492), Granada had time to see its civilisation mature before

🔺 *The mountains of the Sierra Nevada frame the Alhambra at Granada*

being eclipsed. The result is the Alhambra, an exquisite palace-fortress that sits on a hill above the city. The complex is made up of three parts: the fortress or Alcazaba, the summer palace of the Generalife (of interest mainly for its gardens) and the Royal or Nazrid Palace. This last part, an exquisite assembly of patios and intricately decorated halls mostly built in the 14th century, is what everyone comes to see. Visitor numbers are restricted and it is essential to book ahead. **(i)** (902) 22 44 60 **(w)** www.alhambra.org **(l)** 08.30–18.00 Nov–Feb; 08.30–20.00 Mar–Oct

Capilla Real

This exquisite, Gothic royal funerary chapel, which houses the remains of several Spanish kings, is a great place to come for some peace in the middle of the city. Its many decorative features include stunning baroque sculptures. **(a)** C/ Oficios 3 **(i)** (958) 22 92 39 **(w)** www.capillarealgranada.com **(l)** 10.30–13.00, 15.30–18.00 Mon–Sat, 11.00–13.30, 15.30–18.00 Sun. Admission charge

RETAIL THERAPY

Alcaicería Granada's 'Arab market' next to the cathedral has become one large gift shop selling typical Andalucian souvenirs. However, there are a few craft shops of quality such as Artesanía Alcaicería (nos 1, 3 and 10), which specialises in miniature figures for Christmas cribs. **(i)** (958) 22 90 45 **(w)** www.alcaiceria.com **(l)** 10.00–20.30

TAKING A BREAK

Granada is one of the few places in Spain where bars serve a complimentary tapas with each drink – although you can't, of course, choose what you get. Hopping around the bars that

serve the best tapas – some old favourites, some recently opened –
is a popular way to start an evening. You can tell which places serve
the best tapas of the moment because the crowds make it difficult
to get through the door let alone to the bar. Good places to hunt
for authentic tapas bars include the streets around Plaza Nueva
and the streets around Campo del Príncipe. Four long-established
and highly rated tapas bars are as follows.

Bodega Espadafor £ An old-fashioned bar, well known for its tapas.
ⓐ C/ Tinajilla ❶ (958) 20 21 38 🕐 12.00–16.00, 20.00–00.00 Mon–Sat,
June–Sept; 12.00–16.00, 20.00–00.00 Tues–Sun, Oct–May

Bodegas Castañeda £ Near Plaza Nueva. Gets very crowded.
ⓐ Almireceros 1–3 ❶ (958) 21 54 64 🕐 12.00–16.00, 19.00–01.00

Casa Enrique £ Good choice of wines as well as excellent tapas.
ⓐ Acerca del Darro 8 ❶ (958) 25 50 08 🕐 12.00–16.00, 20.00–00.00
Mon–Sat

AFTER DARK

El Camborio With several dance floors, this cave-like bar and
nightclub blasts out R&B, hip hop and rock music until the
early hours. ⓐ Camino del Sacromonte 7 ❶ (958) 22 12 15
ⓦ www.elcamborio.com 🕐 Club: 23.00–07.00 Thur–Sat;
chill-out room: 16.00–21.00 Sat & Sun

Granada-10 A cinema in the evening which becomes a disco
at night, playing disco, hip hop, funk, Latin, salsa – you name it.
ⓐ Carc'él Baja 10 ❶ (958) 22 40 01

OF TOWN

ACCOMMODATION

Casa de Federico ££ A small hotel near the cathedral in which the interior design is a striking and harmonious combination of old and new materials. ➌ C/ Horno de Marina 13 ➊ (958) 20 85 34 Ⓦ www.casadefederico.com

Alhambra Palace £££ A glorious mock-Mooorish building on the same hillside as the Alhambra and with great views from its bar-terrace (open to the public). ➌ Pl. Arquitecto García de Paredes 1 ➊ (958) 22 14 68 Ⓦ www.h-alhambrapalace.es

Palacio de los Patos £££ This swish 5-star boutique hotel with garden and spa is the place to stay in Córdoba. ➌ Solarillo de Gracia 1 ➊ (958) 53 65 16 Ⓦ www.hospes.es

Parador de San Francisco £££ One of the most luxurious hotels in the state-run chain, in a historic building in an incomparable setting beside the Alhambra. It's essential to reserve as far ahead as possible, as it quickly gets booked up. ➌ C/ Real de la Alhambra ➊ (958) 22 14 40 Ⓦ www.parador.es

THE SURROUNDING TOWNS

Antequera

This ancient town at the crossroads between Seville, Granada, Malaga and Córdoba has two clusters of monuments. One is uphill from the tourist information office through a formal 16th-century gateway, the Arco de los Gigantes (Giants' Arch), and includes the Renaissance church of Real Colegiata de Santa María la Mayor and the remains of a Muslim fortress, the Alcazaba.

138

Far older than anything else you will see in Andalucia are three impressive *dólmenes* (dolmens, Neolithic stone formations) on the edge of town. The largest is the Dólmen de Menga, dating, like its neighbour the Dólmen de Viera, from 2500 BC. However, the most interesting is the Dólmen de Romeral because of its domed chamber – the first case of intentional architectural construction in Europe.

Tourist information ⓐ Pl. San Sebastián 7 ⓣ (952) 70 81 42 or 70 25 05 ⓦ www.antequera.es ⓛ 11.00–14.00, 17.00–20.00 Mon–Sat

Dólmenes de Viera, Menga & Romeral ⓐ On the road out towards Archidona ⓛ 09.30–14.30 Tues–Sat

Écija

Écija makes a useful stopover on the way to or from Córdoba. Its main attractions are its 11 churches' baroque steeples. All the main sights can be reached on foot from the main square, the Plaza de España.

Tourist information ⓐ Camino del Físico ⓣ (955) 90 07 21 ⓦ www.turismoecija.com ⓛ 09.30–15.00 Mon–Fri, 10.30–13.30 Sat & Sun

Osuna

Although not very significant today, in the 16th century Osuna was bequeathed a cluster of monumental buildings by the dukes who took their title from it. To explore the most interesting part, head upwards from the Plaza Mayor towards the Renaissance church, which overlooks the town. Down below there is an archaeological museum, the **Museo Arqueológico** (ⓐ Pl. de la Duquesa ⓣ (954) 81 12 07, ⓛ 10.00–13.30, 15.30–18.30 Tues–Sun, Nov–Apr; 10.00–13.30, 16.00–19.00 Tues–Sun, May–Jun & Oct; 10.00–13.30, 16.00–19.00 Tues–Sat,

10.00–13.30 Sun, Jul & Aug; closed Mon), in one of the town's most ancient buildings, the 12th-century Torre del Agua.

Tourist information ⓐ C/ Carrera 82 ❶ (954) 81 57 32 ⓦ www.euosuna.org/turismo ❶ 09.30–13.30, 16.00–18.00 Tues–Sat, 09.00–13.30 Sun

TAKING A BREAK

Casa Curro £ A bar with a good selection of tapas. ⓐ Pl. Salitre 5, Osuna ❶ (955) 82 07 58 ❶ 12.00–00.30 Tues–Sun

AFTER DARK

Caserío de San Benito ££ This very traditional and much-loved restaurant lies a few miles north of Antequera, in the direction of Cordoba. ⓐ Carretera Córdoba–Málaga km 108, Antequera ❶ (952) 11 11 03 ⓦ www.caseriodesanbenito.com ❶ 20.00–00.00 Fri–Sun

ACCOMMODATION

Palacio de los Granados ££ Boutique hotel in a baroque mansion with a small pool in the courtyard. Tapas or a full dinner (on request) served in the evening. ⓐ C/ Emilio Castelar 42, Écija ❶ (955) 90 10 50 ⓦ www.palaciogranados.com

Palacio Marqués de la Gomera ££ Small hotel in an 18th-century aristocratic mansion with a renowned restaurant, La Casa del Marqués. ⓐ C/ San Pedro 20, Osuna ❶ (954) 81 22 23 ⓦ www.hotelpalaciodelmarques.com

---

▶ *A blue tram glides past Seville's cathedral*

PRACTICAL
information

Directory

GETTING THERE

By air

The Aeropuerto de Sevilla (see page 48), located 10 km (6 miles) northeast of the city, is served by a number of scheduled international airlines, four of them flying in from UK airports. Flying time from Britain is around 2½ hours. For details of getting from the airport to the city centre, see page 48.

Spain's national airline **Iberia** (Ⓦ www.iberia.es) flies from London Heathrow and most other European airports, and also operates domestic flights within Spain. Budget airline **Ryanair** (Ⓦ www.ryanair.com) flies to Seville from Bristol, Liverpool and London Stansted, while **Vueling** (Ⓦ www.vueling.com) runs a service to London Heathrow.

Visitor from the USA and other continents must take a connecting flight from Madrid, Barcelona or another European airport.

Many people are aware that air travel emits CO_2, which contributes to climate change. You may be interested in the possibility of lessening the environmental impact of your flight through **Climate Care** (Ⓦ www.climatecare.org), which offsets your CO_2 by funding environmental projects around the world.

By rail

It would take around two days non-stop to reach Seville from London by rail, so this is not a very viable option unless travelling by rail is part of your holiday. The journey time from Madrid on board the high speed AVE (Alta Velocidad Española) train is 2½ hours. Seville's main railway station is Estación de Santa Justa (see page 48).

Mainline and local trains are operated by **RENFE** (☎ (902) 32 03 20
🖊 www.renfe.es).

To plan rail trips around Spain and Europe, check the options offered
by **Rail Europe** (🖊 www.raileurope.co.uk). The *Thomas Cook European
Rail Timetable* (☎ +44 1733 416 477 🖊 www.thomascookpublishing.com)
has up-to-date train timetables for the whole of Europe.

By road

From any of the French Channel ports, head south to Biarritz and cross
the frontier at the western end of the Pyrenees (between Hendaye
and Irún) to reach San Sebastian. Turn inland for Vitoria-Gasteiz and
pick up the A1 motorway for Madrid at Burgos.

Madrid's orbital motorways take some navigating. Arriving from
the north there is no sign saying Seville. The best policy is to go around
Madrid to the east on the M50 following signs first for Zaragoza (but
don't turn off for that city), then Valencia, then Córdoba. If you're
lucky, you'll find yourself heading due south on the A4 motorway
through La Mancha (past Aranjuez) and eventually through the
spectacular pass of Despeñaperros into Andalucia. Follow the signs
for Córdoba and then keep on the same motorway for Seville.

Alternatively, to save driving through France, take a ferry to Bilbao
or Santander (crossing 24–30 hours), and drive south to Burgos, then
on to Madrid.

Driving around the centre of Seville may take some getting
used to and is best avoided in favour of walking and public transport.
Parking can be both difficult and expensive. What's more, some people
choose to double park which makes the traffic problem worse.

Spain drives on the right and its highway code is similar to that
of other European countries, with internationally recognisable traffic

signs. The police can issue on-the-spot fines for traffic offences and being a foreigner does not give you exemption. Seat belts are obligatory and children under 12 should travel in the back.

Speed limits are 120 km/h (74 mph) on motorways, 100 km/h (62 mph) on dual carriageways, 90 km/h (56 mph) on ordinary roads and 50 km/h (31 mph) in built-up areas.

Petrol (*gasolina*) is available as *super*, *normal* (both leaded), *sin plomo* (unleaded) and *gasoil* (diesel).

All the major car-hire companies have offices in Seville (see page 58). Rates are competitive, but you can usually get the best deal by reserving a car from home at the same time as making a flight booking. ❶ When hiring a car you will be asked to show your passport and an EU or international driving licence, as well as a credit (not debit) card

ENTRY FORMALITIES

Most visitors – including citizens of all EU countries, the USA, Canada, Ireland, Australia and New Zealand – require only a valid passport to enter Spain. Visitors from South Africa must have a visa. There is no restriction on what items you may bring in with you as a tourist,

SOME WARNINGS ABOUT DRIVING
Alcohol limits are strict and police are even stricter, so don't be tempted to drink and drive. In your car you must carry two red warning triangles, replacement light bulbs and a reflective jacket in the passenger compartment to wear in case of emergency. If you wear glasses, you must have a spare pair in the car.

but you'll find almost everything you need locally. In Spain you are obliged by law to carry your passport with you all the time in case the police ask for identification.

MONEY

The Spanish currency is the euro. It is divided into 100 cents or *céntimos*. There are coins of 1 and 2 euros, and of 1, 2, 5, 10, 20 and 50 cents. The notes are in denominations of 5, 10, 20, 50, 100, 200 and 500 euros. Banks are generally open only in the morning from 09.00–13.30 Mon–Fri, but there are many cash machines in Seville where you can obtain money with a credit card. Credit cards are accepted for payment almost everywhere except in smaller bars, shops and *pensiones*. Traveller's cheques can be cashed in banks and big hotels. Personal cheques are not accepted anywhere.

HEALTH, SAFETY & CRIME

Although EU citizenship gives you basic health cover in Spain on production of a European Health Insurance Card (EHIC, available online at Ⓦ www.ehic.org.uk), it is advisable to take out personal travel insurance as well. This can be obtained from your travel agent, airline company or any insurance company. Make sure it gives adequate cover not only for medical expenses but also for loss or theft of possessions, personal liability and repatriation in an emergency.

If you are going to Spain by car, ask your insurer for a green card and check with them on the cover you will need for damage, loss or theft of the vehicle and for legal costs in the event of an accident.

If you hire a car you will be asked whether you want to pay extra for collision insurance. You may already be covered for this by your normal UK car insurance.

○ *A mobile police presence makes for a safer city*

Like any big city, Seville has its share of petty crime. That said, most of it is opportunist and a few simple precautions will make sure you are not an easy target.

❶ Watch out for pickpockets in crowed places like markets and bars, and keep your bag across your chest and in front of you.

❶ Leave valuables in a hotel safe, and never leave anything on display in a parked car.

OPENING HOURS

In this famously relaxed region, opening times can be unpredictable. If you are making a special journey to a museum or restaurant, always check precise opening times before you set out.

Shops are usually open 09.00 or 10.00–14.00 and 17.00–20.00, although some re-open later in the afternoon during the heat of high summer. Department stores and supermarkets do not close for the siesta, staying open continuously 10.00–21.00. Shops are generally closed on Sundays except on special occasions such as the run-up to Christmas.

Mealtimes are much later in Spain than in the UK and the rest of Europe. Breakfast in hotels is served 07.30–10.00; lunch is 14.00–16.00; and dinner is generally 21.00–23.00, although dining can go on well past midnight.

Museums and other attractions are generally open 09.00–13.00 and 16.00–20.00 Tuesday to Saturday, and perhaps Sunday morning. They usually close on Mondays. Central post offices open 08.30–20.30 Monday to Friday and 09.30–14.00 on Saturdays, while offices and businesses generally open 09.00–14.00 and 16.00–20.00 Monday to Friday. In the heat of summer, they may simply work a reduced day from 08.00–15.00. Government offices usually don't attend to the public in the afternoon. Banks open 09.00–13.30 on weekdays and are closed at the weekend.

Nightlife is exactly that – at night. Discos and nightclubs don't open until at least 22.00 and go on until 03.00 or sometimes later. Bars and musical venues may open and close slightly earlier and theatres often have two daily performances, one for the early birds at 18.00 and one for night owls at 22.00.

TOILETS

Seville has few public toilets. The most convenient thing to do, therefore, is go into a bar or café – in which case it is polite to buy a drink. Another option is to use those in a department store like El Corte Inglés (see page 69). There are several Spanish words for 'toilets', the most common being *servicios*, *aseos* and *lavabos*.

CHILDREN

In Spain children simply fit into ordinary life. There may not be many special facilities for them, but this lack is more than made up for by a general tolerance and willingness to help. For instance, you are unlikely to see a 'child menu', but you are also unlikely to come across a waiter who won't go out of his way to make sure a child gets something suitable to eat.

If you fancy a nice family outing, try a mooch around the Isla Mágica theme park (see page 95). Most children like quaint forms of transport, and so a river-boat trip (see page 57) or a horse and carriage ride (see page 58) should go down well. If your children are animal fans, head for the best zoo in the region, the **Zoo Botánico** in Jerez (ⓐ C/ Taxdirt, Jeréz de la Frontera ⓣ (956) 14 97 85 ⓦ www.zoobotanicojerez.com). And if all the family feels like some smashing splashing in a cool pool, dive over to **Aquopolis Seville** water park (ⓐ Av. del Deporte, near the Palacio de Congresos, east of the city centre ⓣ (902) 34 50 10 ⓦ www.aquopolis.es/sevilla).

⬤ *The kids will love a trip to the 'Magic Island' theme park*

COMMUNICATIONS

Internet

Seville is as wired as you'd expect any major European city to be, with numerous internet cafés and Wi-Fi hotspots. Ask at your hotel (which should also provide internet access) for the nearest.

Phone

Local, national and international calls can all be made from *cabinas* (public phone booths) in the street, which operate with coins, phone cards or credit cards. *Tarjetas telefónicas* (phone cards) are on sale at *estancos* (tobacconists) and *oficinas de correos* (post offices). You can also phone from *locutorios*, public telephone centres which are quieter and more convenient than phone boxes. Pay at the counter when you have finished your call. Calls from a hotel room are usually very expensive.

TELEPHONING SPAIN

To call Spain from abroad, dial the international access code (00 from the UK, 011 from the US), followed by the country code (34) and phone number, including the full area code (which starts with a 9).

TELEPHONING ABROAD

To call abroad from Spain, dial 00 followed by the relevant country code, area code (usually omitting the first zero if there is one) and the phone number. The country code for the UK is 44, for Ireland 353, for the USA and Canada 1, for Australia 61, for New Zealand 64 and for South Africa 27.

To save high roaming costs, it may be a good idea to buy a Spanish SIM card for your mobile phone. These are available from numerous outlets around town.

The Spanish Yellow Pages is online at
🅦 www.paginasamarillas.es.

Post

Oficinas de Correos (post offices) are usually open 08.30–20.30 Monday to Friday and 09.30–14.00 on Saturdays, although the branch at El Corte Inglés (see page 69) is open longer (🕐 10.00–22.00 Mon–Sat). The main post office is at ❷ Av. de la Constitución 32 ℹ (902) 19 71 97 🅦 www.correos.es. If you just want *sellos* (stamps), however, you can buy them from an *estanco* (tobacconist). Post boxes are bright yellow and often have two slots, one for local mail and one for long-distance and international post. You can find them outside post offices and on many street corners.

ELECTRICITY

Spain's electricity supply is 220 volt, 50 Hz. Plugs have two round pins, so electrical devices from the UK and USA will require an adaptor, easily obtainable at the airport or from an electrical store.

TRAVELLERS WITH DISABILITIES

Travellers with disabilities can obtain a printed copy of the useful *Guía de Turismo Accesible de Sevilla: Sevilla Para Todos* (Seville Accessible Tourism Guide: Seville For All) at the tourist information office (see page 152). Alternatively, you can download a PDF of the guide, along with a map showing accessible tourist routes through the city, from 🅦 www.valinet.org. Unfortunately the guide has not yet been translated into English – try to find a Spanish-speaking friend if you can't understand what it says, or call the tourist office and ask them to check the information. In Seville, wheelchair users are allowed to travel on the cycle paths, which are smoother than the pavements. For more useful links, click on 'Accessible Guide' on Seville's tourist information site Ⓦ www.turismo.sevilla.org.

TOURIST INFORMATION

The **main tourist office** in Seville (Ⓐ Pl. de San Francisco 19 Ⓘ (954) 59 52 88) has the usual leaflets, timetables and information. There are also tourist information offices at the **airport** (Ⓘ (954) 78 20 35) and **Santa Justa** (Ⓘ (954) 78 20 02).

The tourist office for the province of Seville (including Itálica and Carmona) is at Ⓐ Pl. del Triunfo 1–3 Ⓘ (954) 21 00 05. For information about other places in Andalucia – including Jerez, the white villages and towns, Doñana National Park, Córdoba and Granada – contact

COMPLAINTS

Spain has strong consumer laws and a strict order in which to make a complaint. First, explain to the establishment in question why you are unhappy with its product or service. This will usually get results, but if it doesn't your next course of action is to fill in a *hoja de reclamaciones* (official complaints form). That will set in motion an official investigation, but if you want to see what other options you have, contact Seville's **OMIC** (Municipal Consumer Information Office Ⓐ Av. Portugal 2 Ⓘ (954) 23 18 22). If you are still not satisfied, you can apply to the **European Consumer Centre** (Ⓐ Príncipe Vergara 54, 28006 Madrid Ⓘ (918) 22 45 55 Ⓦ http://cec.consumo-inc.es).

the **Junta de Andalucia** (ⓐ Av. de la Constitución 21B ☎ (954) 78 75 78 ⓦ www.andalucia.org). The region's tourist helpline is ☎ (901) 20 00 20.

The official website for Seville is ⓦ www.turismo.sevilla.org. For Spain in general, see ⓦ www.spain.info. Other useful sources of information are ⓦ www.tourspain.co.uk and ⓦ www.andalucia.com.

BACKGROUND READING

Andalucía by Michael Jacobs. If you only read one other book on southern Spain, make it this one.

Andalus: Unlocking the Secrets of Moorish Spain by Jason Webster. A revealing personal interpretation of Spain's 800 years of Moorish influence.

Driving Over Lemons: An Optimist in Andalucia by Chris Stewart. An English family's experiences living on a rural farm in Granada make for fun, light-hearted reading.

Duende: A Journey in Search of Flamenco by Jason Webster. Brush up on the history and meanings behind southern Spain's characteristic form of dance.

Mad Dogs and an English Girl: A Stranger in Franco's Spain by Caroline Waterman. The experiences of an English girl in 1950s Spain under Franco.

The New Spaniards by John Hooper. For background on contemporary Spain, this is a thorough and readable account of social and political change since the death of Franco.

The Seville Communion by Arturo Perez Reverte. A novel that conveys the flavour of the city in which it is set.

Emergencies

The following are emergency free-call numbers:

General emergency ℹ 112
Ambulancia (Ambulance) ℹ 061
Policía nacional (National police) ℹ 091
Policía municipal (Local police) ℹ 092
Guardia Civil (Civil Guard) ℹ 062
Bomberos (Fire brigade) ℹ 080

MEDICAL SERVICES
Ambulances & hospitals
To summon an ambulance ℹ 112
Hospital Universitario Virgen Macarena ⓐ Av. Dr Fedriani
ℹ (955) 00 80 00 (English-speaking doctors available)
Hospital Virgen del Rocío ⓐ Av. Manuel Siurot ℹ (955) 01 20 00
Hospital Virgen de Valme ⓐ Av. Ctra. Sevilla-Cádiz ℹ (955) 01 50 00

Pharmacies
Minor health problems can often be cleared up by consulting a
farmacia, a chemist's shop that is indicated by a green cross sign.
Out of hours, there is always one *farmacia de guardia* open. You'll
find its address posted in the window of other *farmacias*.

POLICE
Seville has three police forces. The Policía Municipal is responsible
for traffic problems and low-level policing. The Policía Nacional
is in charge of more serious crime. The Guardia Civil takes care
of highway patrols and customs. To report a crime in English, call
ℹ (902) 102 112 or visit Seville's **main police station** (ⓐ Av. Blas

Infante 2 ℹ (954) 28 93 00 🌐 www.policia.es).

If you leave an item on a plane, bus or train, contact the company in question and see if it has been handed in. Report the loss of valuable items to a police station. You will need an official form to make an insurance claim.

EMBASSIES & CONSULATES

Australia 🄰 Torre Espacio, Paseo de la Castellana 259D, Madrid
ℹ (91) 353 6600 🌐 www.embaustralia.es
Canada 🄰 Pl. Malagueta 2, Málaga ℹ (952) 22 33 46 🌐 http://spain.gc.ca
Ireland 🄰 Av. de Jerez 46 ℹ (954) 69 06 89 🌐 www.irlanda.es
South Africa 🄰 Edificio Lista, C/ de Claudio Coello 91–6, Madrid
ℹ (91) 436 3780 🌐 www.sudafrica.com
UK 🄰 Edificio Eurocom (south block), C/ Mauricio Moro Pareto 2,
Málaga ℹ (952) 35 23 00 🌐 http://ukinspain.com
US 🄰 C/ Serrano 75, Madrid ℹ (91) 587 2200
🌐 http://madrid.usembassy.gov

EMERGENCY PHRASES

Help!	**Fire!**	**Stop!**
¡Socorro!	¡Fuego!	¡Stop!
¡Sawkoro!	*¡Fwegoh!*	*¡Stop!*

Call an ambulance/a doctor/the police/the fire service!
¡Llame a una ambulancia/un médico/la policía/a los bomberos!
¡Lliame a oona anboolanthea/oon meydico/la poletheea/
a lohs bombehrohs!

Editorial/project management: Lisa Plumridge
Copy editor: Monica Guy
Layout/DTP: Alison Rayner

The publishers would like to thank the following individuals and organisations for supplying their copyright photographs for this book: BigStockPhoto.com (Valeria Cantone, page 122; David Herzog, page 135; Matt Trommer, page 103); Dreamstime.com (Michael Corrigan, page 80; Francisco Javier Alcerreca Gomez, page 13; Jarnogz, page 64; Lorenzo Lesca, pages 40–1; Graça Victoria, page 59); Francisco Javier Alcerreca Gomez/BigStockPhoto.com, page 10; iStockphoto.com (Graham Heywood, page 141; Stephan Hoerold, page 146; Hani Alex Latif, page 9; Roberto A Sanchez, page 89); Sue Anna Joe/SXC.hu, page 70; Alex Lapuerta Mediavilla/123RF, page 101; Turespana, pages 5 & 7; Nick Inman, all others.

Send your thoughts to
books@thomascook.com

- Found a great bar, club, shop or must-see sight that we don't feature?
- Like to tip us off about any information that needs a little updating?
- Want to tell us what you love about this handy little guidebook and more importantly how we can make it even handier?

Then here's your chance to tell all! Send us ideas, discoveries and recommendations today and then look out for your valuable input in the next edition of this title.

Email the above address (stating the title) or write to: pocket guides Series Editor, Thomas Cook Publishing, PO Box 227, Coningsby Road, Peterborough PE3 8SB, UK.

WHAT'S IN YOUR GUIDEBOOK?

Independent authors Impartial up-to-date information from our travel experts who meticulously source local knowledge.

Experience Thomas Cook's 165 years in the travel industry and guidebook publishing enriches every word with expertise you can trust.

Travel know-how Thomas Cook has thousands of staff working around the globe, all living and breathing travel.

Editors Travel-publishing professionals, pulling everything together to craft a perfect blend of words, pictures, maps and design.

You, the traveller We deliver a practical, no-nonsense approach to information, geared to how you really use it.

Useful phrases

English	Spanish	Approx pronunciation
BASICS		
Yes	Sí	*Sí*
No	No	*Noh*
Please	Por favor	*Por fabor*
Thank you	Gracias	*Gratheeas*
Hello	Hola	*Ola*
Goodbye	Adiós	*Adeeos*
Excuse me	Disculpe	*Deeskoolpeh*
Sorry	Perdón	*Pairdohn*
That's okay	De acuerdo	*Dey acwerdo*
I don't speak Spanish	No hablo español	*Noh ahblo espanyol*
Do you speak English?	¿Habla usted inglés?	*¿Ahbla oosteth eengless?*
Good morning	Buenos días	*Bwenos dee-ahs*
Good afternoon	Buenas tardes	*Bwenas tarrdess*
Good evening	Buenas noches	*Bwenas notchess*
Goodnight	Buenas noches	*Bwenas notchess*
My name is ...	Me llamo ...	*Meh lliamo ...*
NUMBERS		
One	Uno	*Oono*
Two	Dos	*Dos*
Three	Tres	*Tres*
Four	Cuatro	*Cwatro*
Five	Cinco	*Thinco*
Six	Seis	*Seys*
Seven	Siete	*Seeyetey*
Eight	Ocho	*Ocho*
Nine	Nueve	*Nwebey*
Ten	Diez	*Deeyeth*
Twenty	Veinte	*Beintey*
Fifty	Cincuenta	*Thincwenta*
One hundred	Cien	*Thien*
SIGNS & NOTICES		
Airport	Aeropuerto	*Aehropwerto*
Rail station	Estación de trenes	*Estatheeon de trenes*
Platform	Vía	*Veea*
Smoking/ Non-smoking	Fumadores/ No fumadores	*Foomadoores/ No foomadoores*
Toilets	Servicios	*Serbeetheeos*
Ladies/Gentlemen	Señoras/Caballeros	*Senyoras/Kaballieros*
Metro/Tram/Bus	Metro/Tranvía/Autobús	*Mehtro/Tranvee-ah/ Awtoeboos*